Lecture Notes on Sexually Transmitted Diseases

R. NICOL THIN

MD FRCPE

Consultant Physician
Department of Genito-urinary Medicine
St. Thomas' Hospital, London

BLACKWELL SCIENTIFIC PUBLICATIONS

OXFORD LONDON EDINBURGH
BOSTON MELBOURNE

© 1982 by
Blackwell Scientific Publications
Editorial offices:
Osney Mead, Oxford, OX2 0EL
8 John Street, London, WC1N 2ES
9 Forrest Road, Edinburgh, EH1 2QH
52 Beacon Street, Boston,
  Massachusetts 02108, USA
99 Barry Street, Carlton,
  Victoria 3053, Australia

First published 1982

Typeset by
Scottish Studios & Engravers Ltd,
Glasgow
Printed and bound in Great Britain by
Billing and Sons Ltd,
Guildford, London, Oxford,
Worcester

DISTRIBUTORS

USA
  Blackwell Mosby Book
  Distributors,
  11830 Westline Industrial Drive,
  St. Louis, Missouri 63141

Canada
  Blackwell Mosby Book
  Distributors,
  120 Melford Drive, Scarborough,
  Ontario, M1B 2X4

Australia
  Blackwell Scientific Book
  Distributors,
  214 Berkeley Street, Carlton,
  Victoria 3053

British Library
Cataloguing in Publication Data
Thin, R. Nicol
  Lecture notes on sexually
    transmitted diseases.
  1. Venereal diseases
  I. Title
  619.95'1   RC200

  ISBN 0-632-008342

Lecture Notes on

Sexually Transmitted Diseases

Contents

Preface

This book is primarily intended for undergraduate medical students, but I hope it will be of value to postgraduates. In addition I hope it will be useful to staff in sexually transmitted disease clinics and in schools of nursing.

While there has been a decline in the incidence of syphilis in the western world, this disease is still common in many other areas. Its relative rarity in the West sometimes leads to errors in diagnosis and management. I have therefore covered syphilis in reasonable detail. The rapidly changing antimicrobial sensitivity of *Neisseria gonorrhoeae* has lead to problems in the treatment of gonorrhoea, and the regimens recommended here may change.

It gives me great pleasure to thank all those who helped me so much in the preparation of this book, especially Cathie Slatter BA(HONS.), MMAA, IMBI, who undertook all the artwork, Dr Paul D. Simmons MB, MRCP, who read the whole manuscript, and Michele Henry who did most of the typing. Richard Zorab of Blackwells has been a great source of encouragement and help. Finally I thank my wife and family for their forebearance while I have been writing the book.

R. Nicol Thin
London

September 1981

CHAPTER 1

Introduction

Venereal diseases regulations

The Venereal Diseases Regulations of 1916 provided the framework for the nationwide network of clinics which developed in Britain after the First World War. They stated that treatment was to be:
>   confidential,
>   free of charge,

and the Venereal Diseases (VD) were:
>   syphilis,
>   gonorrhoea,
>   chancroid.

These principles still apply and Britain still has one of the most comprehensive clinic services in the world. Syphilis, gonorrhoea and chancroid remain the legally defined venereal diseases.

Sexually transmitted diseases

Until the end of the Second World War most of the patients attending the Venereal Diseases Clinics, or 'Special Clinics' as they were often called, had syphilis, gonorrhoea and, to a declining extent, chancroid. After the War patients began to attend in increasing numbers with other conditions.

Men came with	non-gonococcal urethritis.
Women came with	vaginal discharges due to:
	trichomoniasis,
	candidosis.

Men and women came with viral conditions such as:
>   warts,
>   genital herpes simplex,
>   genital molluscum contagiosum.

and parasitic conditions such as:
>   scabies,
>   pediculosis.

It was considered helpful to replace the name *Venereal* with a similar term with less stigma attached to it, so the name *Sexually Transmitted Diseases* (STDs) was introduced and is now used in many parts of the world.

Genito-urinary medicine

In recent years patients have come to STD clinics with an ever wider range of problems such as:
>   requests for examination to exclude infection,
>   requests to exclude infection as a possible cause of subfertility,
>   non-infective conditions of the genitals and nearby.

It has been realised that in some groups conditions such as:
>   hepatitis B,
>   intestinal infestations

may be sexually acquired.

It was therefore considered useful to devise another name to reflect the widening range of conditions and the expanding horizons of the doctors, so the name *Genito-Urinary Medicine* was chosen. While far from ideal it does at least get away from the narrow-minded stigma of VD. But note that some specialists in the UK prefer to regard the term *Venereology* as embracing all the recent concepts of genito-urinary medicine.

Lay-out and work in a clinic

The work in a clinic is often regarded as mysterious as a result of the stigma which used to be attached to the venereal diseases. In fact, the work in the old venereal disease clinic as in the modern genito-urinary medicine department is simply the practice of good medicine. This is achieved by a high standard of clinical examination and laboratory investigation leading to:
>   rapid accurate diagnosis,
>   effective treatment,

tracing at-risk sexual contacts,
careful follow-up to ensure treatment is effective,
tracing defaulters from follow-up
accurate record keeping.
For this work the following rooms or areas are needed:
reception office with document storage space,
doctors' interviewing rooms,
examination rooms,
investigation area,
laboratory,
treatment area,
contact tracer's room,
social worker's room,
waiting areas,
additional accommodation.

Staff

It follows that in addition to doctors and nurses the full staff of a clinic should include:
receptionists,
secretary
contact tracer, often in the UK called Health Worker, or Health Adviser,
social worker.

In most clinics in the UK the nurses undertake staining and microscopy. If not, it may be necessary to have a technician for this work.

The rooms and areas in the clinic

Reception

Most clinics operate an open-door policy so that patients can attend without an appointment whenever the clinic is open. This means that patients' documents must be immediately available within the clinic. Furthermore, in most clinics the extra confidentiality implied by the Venereal Diseases Regulations of 1916 is taken to mean that the documents do not leave the clinic at any time.

The receptionist, who is usually the first member of the staff the patient meets, has an important role in putting patients at their ease. It is important to obtain accurate personal particulars from the patients so that if need be they can be contacted, and sexual partners can be matched. Furthermore, if the receptionist develops a good rapport with the patient it is easier for the rest of the staff to do so.

Once the personal details are taken the patient is asked to wait in the waiting room until called by the doctor into the Interviewing Room.

Interviewing room

This should be bright, cheerful, comfortable and soundproof. The doctor needs to know intimate details concerning the patient's medical and sexual contact history. It is important that the patient should feel there is an atmosphere of privacy in order to relax and talk easily.

Examination room

A feeling of privacy is again important. Examination usually concentrates on patients' genitals, and co-operation is best obtained if the atmosphere is warm and the patient is comfortable and relaxed. Once clinical examination is complete the necessary swabs and blood samples may be taken on the spot or the patient may be asked to dress and move to the investigation area. With female patients, examination and the collection of genital specimens is usually combined. With male patients the two procedures may be separate. The female is usually examined in the lithotomy position. Facilities and equipment should be available for full clinical examination.

Investigation area

As in other areas, privacy is essential where genital samples are taken. Male patients should lie on a couch. There should be a lavatory where urine samples can be passed. It is often more convenient to take venous blood from a patient sitting in a chair, but a couch should be nearby for the occasional patient who has a syncopal attack.

Laboratory area

This area should have facilities for:
    Gram staining,
    microscopy,
    centrifuging urine.
In addition, there should be an incubator and a refrigerator.
    There must be supplies of:
    electricity,
    water,
    gas.
Whenever possible, one microscope should be kept fitted with a dark-ground (field) condenser; this is much more convenient than changing the condenser whenever dark-ground microscopy is needed.

Treatment room

Most clinics in the UK keep supplies of the drugs commonly prescribed. This:
    ensures that the patient receives the treatment,
    saves the embarrassment of attending a pharmacy where other
        patients are paying for their treatment.
These supplies should be kept locked. There should be a couch for patients receiving injections. The room should be soundproof so that the details of administration of vaginal pessaries can be described in privacy. There should be a supply of drinking water so that doses of tablets can be taken at once under supervision.

Contact tracer's and social worker's rooms

The rooms where the contact tracers and social workers see patients should be soundproof and should look cheerful.

Waiting areas

These should be bright, cheerful, well furnished and have up-to-date magazines.

Lay-out of rooms

Few clinics are purpose built, and in most the best use has to be made of the accommodation which is available. It is important that the rooms and areas should be arranged so that the patient can move easily from room to room in the order they have been described (see Fig. 1.1). The staff also need to be able to move around freely without inconveniencing each other or the patients.

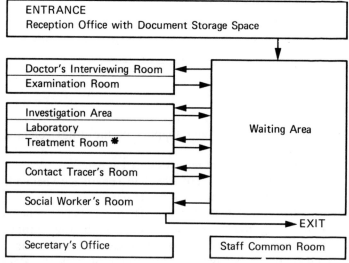

FIG. 1.1   Flow chart to show progress of a patient through a typical clinic.* Patients return to doctor to be told results of investigations and treatment needed before going to treatment room.

Additional accommodation

Additional accommodation needed includes:
     secretary's office,
     a staff rest room or common room,
     staff lavatories,
     a teaching or meeting room,
     access to a suitable number and range of specialist and general
          textbooks and journals.

Siting of clinic

All clinics should be situated in a general hospital near the:
main entrance,
casualty (accident and emergency) department,
other out-patient clinics,
microbiology laboratories,
medical wards.

CHAPTER 2

Epidemiology and control

Epidemiology

Syphilis

Apart from a marked peak during the Second World War, there was a steady fall in the number of cases of syphilis notified in Britain from 1925 to 1955 (Fig. 2.1). Thereafter the number remained at a fairly steady low level with a slight increase in men in the 1970s. This is mainly due to an increase in primary and secondary syphilis in homosexuals. In the late 1970s there was a smaller increase in women. Congenital syphilis remains rare in Britain.

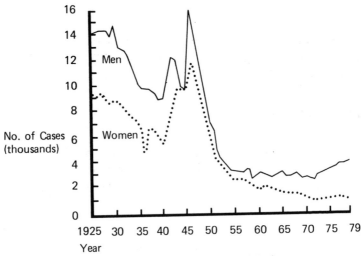

FIG. 2.1   New cases of syphilis in Britain.

Care should be taken comparing figures in one country with those in another because of differences in recording systems. Syphilis is uncommon in Britain compared with many countries.

Gonorrhoea

The pattern for gonorrhoea in Britain is shown in Fig. 2.2. Note the difference in the vertical scale between Fig. 2.2 and Fig. 2.1. The trend for gonorrhoea resembles that for syphilis between 1925 and 1955, but thereafter gonorrhoea increased dramatically until about 1970 when it levelled out and then remained fairly steady. However, it is lower than in many countries.

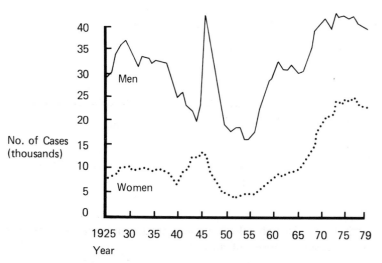

FIG. 2.2 New cases of gonorrhoea in Britain.

Non-specific urethritis

Non-specific urethritis in men has increased dramatically since it was first recorded separately in Britain in 1951 and the increase continued, though at a slower rate, during the 1970s (Fig. 2.3).

Other sexually transmitted diseases

Most other commonly sexually transmitted diseases such as

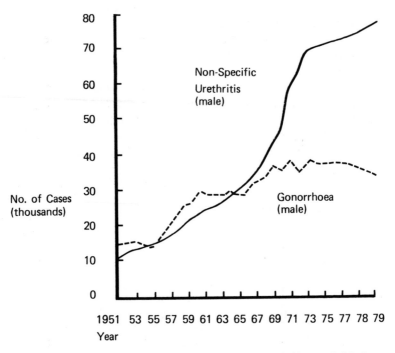

FIG. 2.3   New cases of gonococcal and non-specific urethritis in Britain.

trichomoniasis, pediculosis, genital herpes and genital warts have all increased recently in England.

Factors associated with high and rising figures for sexually transmitted diseases

Fundamental factors

There are two fundamental factors:
1. acquisition of infection from one partner and transmission to another,
2. availability of multiple sexual partners.

Other factors may be divided into medical and social.

Medical factors

Women with asymptomatic disease,
homosexual men with asymptomatic disease, especially
syphilis and gonorrhoea.
modern treatment:
> simple, quick, effective, so may encourage risk of infection,
> *but* antimicrobial resistance leads to treatment failure and
> spread of infection.

modern contraceptives:
> intrauterine devices and oral contraceptives bar the sperm
> but not the germ, unlike the old barrier   contraceptives,
> the sheath and diaphragm.

Social factors

Population movement:
> throughout the world from rural to urban areas,
> between towns and countries.

increasing affluence,
alcohol consumption,
leisure time,
personal freedom in the West—spreading to other countries,
prostitution,
ignorance:
> failure to recognise infection,
> continuing partner change despite infection.

High risk groups

Age groups:
> 20–24 years for both sexes,
> 20–34 years for men,
> 16–24 years for women,

frequent travellers,
prostitutes,
homosexuals,
members of the armed forces, merchant navy, air crew,
entertainers before the public and in supporting services.

Note that these infections affect all socio-economic groups: no one
is immune.

Control

In Britain there are three main branches to control:
1. the clinics,
2. contact tracing,
3. education.

Screening, e.g. of blood donors and antenatal women, is also important, but more cases are found by screening in some other countries than in Britain.

The clinics

The clinics provide the foundation of control in Britain. The work of the clinic is good medical practice and comprises:
1. accurate diagnosis by clinical examination and laboratory investigation for all the common diseases,
2. effective treatment,
3. follow-up to ensure treatment is effective,
4. contact tracing (to be considered below),
5. in addition, returns of numbers of cases so clinic services can be adjusted to meet demand.

Contact tracing

Contact tracers, or health workers, as they are often called in Britain, must:
1. interview the patient to:
   a. ensure the patient has an adequate knowledge of the condition to co-operate,
   b. establish the at-risk contacts,
   c. motivate the patient to persuade contacts to attend for examination and, if necessary, treatment,
   d. re-interview the patient when attending for follow-up to check on the progress of contact action and see if he has remembered more contacts,
2. secure the attendance of defaulters from follow-up—such default does not imply cure,
3. occasionally go out into the community to find:
   defaulters,
   contacts.

Contact tracers must be:
    tactful,
    dedicated,
    persevering,
    courageous,
    resourceful.
Good contact tracers develop important links in their local community with people such as:
    publicans,
    club managers,
    community social workers,
    other social service workers,
    probation officers.

Education

Clinical work and contact tracing only play their part in control of sexually transmitted disease once the patient comes to a clinic. It is important that the public know:
1. clinical features of the common diseases,
2. how the diseases are acquired,
3. where to find the clinics,
4. that treatment at a clinic is free and confidential,
5. attendance at a clinic is similar to attendance at any other outpatient department.

Fortunately, more and more people are coming to accept the last statement; sadly there are still people who do not.

It is even more important that doctors and other health workers should regard attendance at a sexually transmitted diseases clinic as similar to attendance at any other outpatient clinic. It is to assist this acceptance and to reflect the ever-widening range of conditions and problems with which patients present, that many clinics in Britain have changed their name to Departments of Genito-Urinary Medicine.

These measures alone will not control the spread of infection. It is necessary to emphasise the importance of minimising sexual partner change. This principle has not yet had enough publicity.

Where and when to educate the public is another problem

In theory, the best place is in school where:

almost everyone can be reached,

information can be provided before sexual maturity occurs. Unfortunately, this is not yet accepted by all school authorities.

If such education is left until after leaving school, it is impossible to reach everyone. Furthermore, the well-motivated people who can be reached through clubs or voluntary attendance at lectures at work or during tertiary education probably find out for themselves from books or leaflets. The less well motivated do not find out for themselves and do not attend lectures. Television, though a potent method of disseminating information has not so far been useful in STD education.

Male homosexuals—a problem group

Men who have sexual contact solely with other men are homosexuals and those who have sexual contact with men and women are bisexuals. No one knows just what proportion of men are homosexual or bisexual at any one time. Furthermore, no one knows how sexually active all these men are. Homosexuals and bisexuals congregate in large cities. The staff working in clinics serving these areas are aware that some of these men have many contacts and frequent infections. Often homosexuals know little or nothing about their contacts.

As already stated, homosexuals have a high prevalence of syphilis (primary, secondary and early latent), gonorrhoea, and hepatitis B (Australia antigen).

The reasons for this are not clear, but may be related to the greater anorectal trauma which occurs in homosexual intercourse than in most forms of heterosexual intercourse. In some areas homosexuals and bisexuals also have a high prevalence of enteric disease and intestinal infestations.

It follows that homosexuals and bisexuals should be especially carefully examined. Dark-ground examinations must be performed in all:

> genital,
> anorectal,
> anopharyngeal lesions,

while lesions at other sites must be viewed with higher than usual suspicion.

Smears and cultures should be taken routinely from the rectum as well as the urethra and a culture taken from the pharynx. Stool examination by microscopy and culture should be considered.

Serum should be examined for Hepatitis B antigen (HBs Ag) as well as antitreponemal antibodies.

When the contact history is taken it should be remembered that the patient may have had very many contacts. He may be embarrassed to admit his sexual orientation and his lack of knowledge about his sexual partners.

It is good practice to encourage homosexuals to attend for regular examination every 3–6 months.

Homosexuals will be considered again in Chapter 19.

CHAPTER 3

Clinical examination

Clinical examination in a clinic is based on the principles of clinical examination in any other department. There is emphasis on genital and related features. The principles are:

1. history,
2. physical examination,
3. collection of samples for laboratory investigations and their transport to the laboratory in optimum condition.

History

This includes:

history of present illness,

general health,

recent treatment, topical and systemic with particular reference to antibiotics,

sexual contacts including marital and extramarital, regular and casual, genital, oral and rectal, and in men, heterosexual and homosexual contacts must be considered (though direct questioning early in an interview is best avoided),

past history of STD and other genital or related disease,

past history of other serious illness,

family history,

drug hypersensitivity,

and in women, menstrual history, pregnancies and their outcome.

Care and tact must be exercised in eliciting this information and the inexperienced clinician needs to work hard to develop the technique of history taking. Patients should be allowed to tell their story in their own words, and leading questions should be avoided as far as possible. Particular care is necessary in eliciting the sexual contact history. It is important for the doctor to avoid any emotional response to details of the patient's history.

Physical examination

Men

The first time a patient attends a complete physical examination should be undertaken if time permits. This and reasons for it should be explained to the patient so he understands what is happening. He should take off all his clothes apart from his underpants and lie on a comfortable couch under a good light. The ordinary routine for clinical examination should be followed.

In younger patients in whom syphilis or superficial infestations are likely, special attention should be given to:
   skin, including body hair
   lymph nodes,
   perianal region,
   mouth, teeth and pharynx.
In older patients, care should be taken in examining:
   pupils,
   optic fundi,
   central nervous system,
   cardiovascular system.
The patient should then be asked to remove his underpants. The genital examination techniques used are inspection and palpation. The inguinal and suprapubic regions should be inspected first, then the penis, the prepuce retracted and the underlying parts inspected, and then the meatus. Finally inspect the scrotum and palpate the contents.

If a urethral discharge is present its colour and consistency should be noted. Samples must then be taken for microbiological investigations. First the meatus is wiped with a clean, dry cottonwool ball or gauze swab. Material for smear and culture may be collected with a platinum or plastic loop, or a cottonwool swab (Fig. 3.1). A smear is made on a clean glass microscope slide.

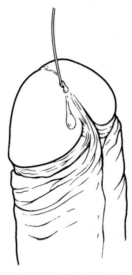

FIG. 3.1   Collection of urethral discharge from urethral meatus with a wire loop.

The material for culture for *Neisseria gonorrhoeae* may be inoculated:

> on to a growth medium (see Table 3.4),
>
> or on to a growth and transport medium such as Transgrow or similar media (see Table 3.4),
>
> or into a transport medium such as Stuart's or Amies' (Table 3.4).

In certain circumstances, as in a man who is a contact, even when no discharge is obviously present, it is important to insert a loop or swab into the meatus to try to obtain material for microbiological investigation. A smear is then made and a culture inoculated as outlined. First, gently massage secretion down the urethra towards the meatus, *but* explain to the patient he should *not* do this to see if he has a discharge. Massage or squeezing can irritate the urethra, produce a discharge and delay healing.

Where facilities are available a urethral swab should be taken for culture for *Chlamydia trachomatis*. Fine cottonwool swabs mounted on wire should be used. They should be inserted slowly into the urethra for several centimetres. The swab is then cut off into a capsule of chlamydia transport medium.

Swabs may also be taken from the meatus for mycoplasma and ureaplasma and placed in Stuart's medium. If all these swabs are to be taken from one patient, they should be in the order gonococci, mycoplasma and chlamydia, each swab being inserted a little further than the preceeding one.

If urethral trichomoniasis is suspected then a loop must be passed about 2 cm into the urethra and gently scraped against the mucosa. The material obtained is then mixed with a drop of saline on a slide for immediate microscopy for the flagellate parasite *Trichomonas vaginalis*. A further scrape is then taken and the material inoculated into a bottle of trichomonas culture medium for immediate incubation.

If there is any inflammation of the glans penis (balanitis) or the under surface of prepuce (posthitis; the two together being called balanoposthitis but often loosely called balanitis) then further samples should be taken.

Material should be collected from any moist areas and/or the coronal sulcus with a loop, mixed with a drop of physiological saline on a slide and examined microscopically for trichomonads. As above, material for culture for trichomonads should also be taken. Material should also be taken with a loop or cotton swab and placed on a slide for Gram stain and microscopy for yeasts *(Candida albicans)*, and a Sabouraud dextrose agar slope should also be inoculated for culture for candida species.

The investigations are summarised in Table 3.1.

The patient should then pass urine into two conical glasses up to a depth of 5 cm in the first and the remainder in the second.

The urine in the first glass should be inspected visually for:

a general haze which is due to suspended leucocytes and indicates acute urethritis,

small specks which may indicate fairly acute inflammation in the urethral ducts and glands (of Littre),

longer threads which may indicate more chronic inflammation in the ducts.

If the first glass is unexpectedly found to contain these abnormalities then it can be centrifuged and specimens for microscopy and culture can be collected from the deposit.

If there is very active urethritis the urine in the second glass may have a slight haze, but usually in urethritis the urine in the second glass is clear. Changes in the urine in the second glass may indicate disease of the upper urinary tract, namely bladder, ureters or kidneys. If this is suspected, a midstream sample of urine should be collected and sent to the laboratory for culture.

Cloudy urine in both glasses indicates phosphaturia which can be cleared by the addition of dilute acetic acid. Cloudy urine containing phosphates is whiter than the hazy urine of acute urethritis.

The urine in the second glass should be tested for sugar and protein at every patient's first visit.

The perineum and anus must be inspected in all men and, in homosexuals the rectum should be examined. The patient should kneel on the couch in the knee–elbow position. The anus should be examined for ulcers, discharge, fissures, fistulae or haemorrhoids. A proctoscope should be passed, using only a little lubricant, and the rectum inspected. Any inflammatory exudate should be collected for a smear for leucocytes and Gram-negative intracellular diplococci, and culture for gonococci. If no exudate is visible, the swab or loop should be rubbed gently against the rectal mucosa. It is a good plan to keep this swab or loop ready in the instrument as it is slowly withdrawn and any exudate that appears can be collected. Whenever proctoscopy is undertaken in a clinic, for whatever reason, material for smear and culture should be collected. Whenever an anal condition such as warts is noted proctoscopy must be performed.

In homosexuals, many of whom have orogenital contact, and in heterosexuals who admit to this practice, a throat swab should be taken for culture for gonococci, and other pathogens if there is tonsillitis or pharyngitis. There is no point in taking a smear as the saprophytic neisseria species in the pharynx cause confusion.

Women

While the man can see what is going on during a genital examination the woman cannot. It is therefore most important, before she has her first examination, to explain to a woman what it entails. Examination consists of inspection and palpation. Before any part is touched the examiner should tell the patient what is about to happen. A nurse should always be present.

The patient should be examined in the lithotomy position. The skin should be inspected over the:

    inguinal regions,
    suprapubic area,

thighs,
perineum,
perianal region,
vulva.

The pubic hair must be inspected for lice. The inguinal regions are palpated for nodes. The labia minora should be parted and the introitus carefully examined. Any discharge should be wiped off and any exudate from the urethral meatus noted; if exudate is seen, material for smear and culture should be collected.

Each labium major should then be palpated between a gloved finger and thumb for thickening of Bartholin's gland: if this is present, the opening of the duct should be carefully examined. A smear and culture should be made from any discharge present; if there is no obvious discharge the duct and gland should be carefully massaged.

A vaginal speculum moistened only with water is then inserted

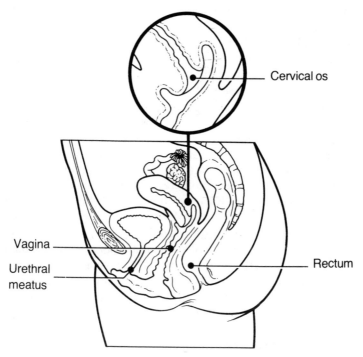

FIG. 3.2 Sagittal section through female pelvis to show anatomy and sites for collection of specimens for routine investigations.

and the ectocervix identified and its appearance noted. The cervical os and any discharge are noted. The vaginal walls are then inspected and the amount and quality of discharge noted.

The following samples should then be taken:

secretion from the lateral vaginal walls for smear and culture for yeasts,

secretion from the posterior fornix for wet film and culture for trichomonads,

cervical smear from around the cervical os for Papanicolaou staining.

Then after wiping the cervical os free of vaginal secretion:

collect material from the cervical os for smear and culture for leucocytes and organisms.

The vaginal speculum should now be withdrawn. If there is no overt urethritis, the tip should be run along the anterior vaginal wall as it is withdrawn to massage any infected secretion towards the meatus for smear and culture. Many women find this uncomfortable, so care should be taken to tell them in advance of what is about to happen. Sometimes the meatus is difficult to see, but it usually opens as the speculum is inserted so look for it then.

When gonorrhoea is suspected, a proctoscope should be passed as in the men and material collected for smear and culture.

These investigations are summarised in Table 3.2.

Men and women

Examination of ulcers

The size, shape and position of any ulcer on or near the genitals should be noted, as should the degree of tenderness. The base of the ulcer must be palpated for induration (thickening). The regional lymph nodes should be examined for enlargement, including size, mobility, tenderness and overlying redness.

The most important cause of any genital ulcer is primary syphilis. Dark-ground (field) examination for the causative organism, *Treponema pallidum*, is necessary to establish or disprove this diagnosis. The following steps are required for this procedure:

thoroughly clean the ulcer with physiological saline,

abrade it with a rough gauze swab,

squeeze between gloved finger and thumb,

mop off any blood,

collect any serum with a coverslip held in Coronet forceps.

If insufficient serum is obtained:

abrade the margin of the ulcer either with a sterile scarifier or scalpel blade,

squeeze again and collect serum with a coverslip,

press coverslip firmly on a clean glass slide 1 mm thick,

examine with a microscope with a dark-ground condenser.

If the result is negative, the examination should be repeated on three consecutive days. During this time the only topical application should be physiological saline, and treponemacidal antimicrobials must be avoided.

A genital ulcer may also be due to herpes simplex virus (HSV). In all cases a culture for HSV should be taken after the dark-ground examination. A swab should be scraped firmly around the base of the ulcer and broken off into a bottle of virus transport medium such as Hank's medium. In women it is good practice to take a swab for viral culture from the cervical os whenever a swab is taken from a genital ulcer.

These investigations are summarised in Table 3.3.

Serological tests

At their first visit a sample of venous blood should be taken from all patients to test for serum antibodies such as the VDRL and TPHA antibodies produced in treponemal disease. In homosexuals and certain other high-risk groups, such as drug addicts, take blood for Hepatitis B (Australia) antigen tests.

Transport of specimens to the laboratory

It is essential that specimens reach the laboratory in the best possible condition.

Gonococcal cultures require particularly careful handling. If swabs are plated on to growth medium this must be placed straight into a candle extinction jar which is put in an incubator at 36°C. If it has to be moved, the whole jar should be taken and transit time should be as short as possible.

Stuart's and Amies' media should reach the laboratory within 24 hours for the best results.

Sabouraud cultures can be left for long periods.

Herpes virus cultures in Hank's medium should be taken straight to the laboratory for inoculation on to cell culture growth medium for the best results.

Swabs for chlamydia should ideally be inoculated straight on to cell culture growth medium. If this is not possible, then special transport medium should be used and the capsule should be placed straight into liquid nitrogen.

Similarly, swabs for mycoplasma culture should be inoculated on to growth medium as soon as possible.

If blood samples cannot be taken to the laboratory within a few hours, the serum should be separated.

TABLE 3.1 Summary of routine investigations in men.

Problem	Investigations
Urethral discharge	Smear—Gram stain for leucocytes and organisms, Wet film for trichomonads, Culture for gonococci, Culture for trichomonads, (If available: Culture for chlamydia, culture for ureaplasma after samples for microbiological examination have been taken.)
Balanitis/ balanoposthitis	Smear for Gram stain for leucocytes and yeasts, Culture for candida species, Wet film for trichomonads, Culture for trichomonads, Swab for aerobic and anaerobic bacteria, Occasionally, cultures for: Herpes virus, Haemophilus ducreyi.
Suspected rectal infection, e.g. anal warts	Smear—Gram stain for leucocytes and organisms, Culture for gonococci.
Suspected throat infection	Culture for gonococci.
Homosexuals bisexuals	Blood for Hepatitis B (Australia) antigen, Rectal smear and culture for gonococci, Throat culture for gonococci.
ALL CASES	BLOOD FOR SERUM ANTIBODIES (VDRL and TPHA) Urine two glass test for macroscopic examination, Microscopic examination of centrifuged deposit for leucocytes, trichomonads and organisms, Urinanalysis.

TABLE 3.2 Summary of routine investigations in women. The following investigations should be collected from all new female patients.

Site	Investigation
Vagina	Smear from lateral wall— Gram stain for yeasts and Culture for candida species, Wet film from posterior fornix for trichomonads, Culture from posterior fornix for trichomonads.
Cervical os	Smear—Gram stain for leucocytes and organisms, Culture for gonococci, Smear for cytological examination, (If available: Cultures for chlamydia, ureaplasma and mycoplasma.)
Urethral meatus	Smear—Gram stain for leucocytes and organisms, Culture for gonococci.
ALL CASES	BLOOD FOR SERUM ANTIBODIES (VDRL and TPHA) Urinanalysis

In gonorrhoea contacts:

Site	Investigation
Rectum	Smear—Gram stain for leucocytes and organisms, Culture for gonococci.
Throat	Culture for gonococci after oro-genital contact.

TABLE 3.3 Investigation of a genital ulcer.

Dark ground examination of serum (daily for at least three days),
Swab for herpes virus culture,
In addition, in women, a swab from the cervical os for herpes virus cultures.

TABLE 3.4 Gonococcal media.

Transport media	Stuart's, Amies'.
Transport and growth media	Transgrow, Neigon–Jembec, Micro-cult-GC.

Growth media:
  Unselecive
    (No antimicrobials)
	Chocolate or heated blood agar,

Selective (Various antimicrobials)	Thayer Martin, Philip's.

CHAPTER 4

Early acquired syphilis

Syphilis

Definition

Syphilis is: chronic,
infectious,
systemic from the beginning.
There are: florid manifestations at some times,
long periods of latency at other times.
It is: transferable to the fetus *in utero*.
And it: responds to treatment with penicillin.

Causative organism

Treponema pallidum is one of the pathogenic treponemes which infect man. They are all indistinguishable morphologically and serologically at present. They are all spirochaetes which can be subdivided as shown in Table 4.1.

Treponema pallidum (Fig. 4.1)

T. pallidum is a tiny spiral-shaped organism with the following characteristics:
Length: 5–20 or more μm
Breadth: 0·25 μm
No. of coils: 5—20
Amplitude of coil approximately 1 μm

TABLE 4.1   Spirochaetes.

TREPONEMATA
Pathogenic:
    T. pallidum of venereal syphilis,
    T. pallidum of endemic syphilis,
    T. pertenue of yaws,
    T. carateum of pinta.
Saprophytic:
    T. macrodentium found in the mouth,
    T. microdentium found in the mouth.
Special strains including:
    Nichols strain of *T. pallidum* which is pathogenic.

BORRELIA
Including:
    B. gracilis,
    B. refringens,
    B. balantidis.
All may be found in subpreputial discharges.

LEPTOSPIRA
Including:
    L. icterohaemorrhagica,
    L. canicola.

MORPHOLOGY

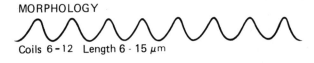

Coils 6 - 12   Length 6 - 15 μm

MOTILITY

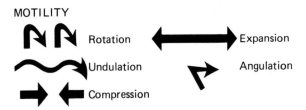

FIG. 4.1   Morphology and motility of *Treponema pallidum*. Note the regularity of the coils.

T. pallidum can be seen in serum from a primary or secondary lesion under a microscope fitted with a dark-ground condenser and a ×40–100 objective with oil immersion. It can be distinguished from other organisms by the regular shape of its coils and by its far greater activity (Fig. 4.1), it shows:

> rotation and forward movement,
> coil compression and expansion,
> undulation,
> and, most characteristically, angulation.

Microscopic recognition is important as the organisms cannot be cultured on artificial media such as agar or cell culture. It can be grown by animal inoculation but this is only suitable for experimental studies. Saprophytic treponemes are less active, smaller or larger, and the coils are less regular.

Classification of venereal syphilis

The two main divisions of venereal syphilis are:

> acquired,
> congenital.

Sub-divisions of acquired syphilis

These are:

Early	primary,
	secondary,
	early latent.
Late	late latent,
	tertiary,
	cardiovascular,
	neurosyphilis.

Sub-divisions of congenital syphilis

These are:

> early,
> late,
> stigmata or scars.

The dividing line between early and late syphilis, in both congenital and acquired forms is arbitrarily placed at 2 years (though occasionally it is extended to 4 years). This 2-year division is chosen because the lesions during the first 2 years contain many treponemes and are infectious. During the incubation period and during the early latent stage the disease may also be infectious.

Late syphilis

In the late stage there are very few treponemes, and the disease is not infectious.

Tertiary syphilis is now rare in the Western areas of the world. The lesions take about 10 years to develop. The pathological lesion is a granuloma called a gumma, and another name for this stage is benign gummatous syphilis as this stage runs a benign course.

This is in contrast to cardiovascular and neurosyphilis which are more dramatic and may be fatal. They are regarded by some as part of tertiary syphilis, but in view of the contrast in their behaviour it seems more logical to regard them as quarternary syphilis.

Before the penicillin era it was shown that 60 per cent of all patients reaching late latent syphilis remained in that stage without treatment unless another illness, such as tuberculosis, developed which reduced the patient's immunity.

The natural history of congenital syphilis resembles that of acquired syphilis except:
1. There is no primary stage,
2. The late stages develop approximately 20 years sooner than in acquired syphilis.

It is important to understand the classification of syphilis for it and the definition provide the framework for the theoretical understanding of the disease. It is also important to classify each case as soon as possible after diagnosis to:
1. prescribe the correct treatment,
2. trace the right contacts,
3. give the right advice concerning,
   a. sexual intercourse,
   b. marriage,
   c. reproduction.

These are all vitally important for the individual patient. Often, classification is easy, as in primary and secondary syphilis. In latent syphilis it may be much more difficult.

Many patients are discovered following routine serological screening and some give no history of a primary or secondary stage.

It is not clear in such patients whether the early clinical stages are unnoticed or do not occur.

Histopathology of syphilis

The basic changes are essentially the same in all stages of syphilis. There is perivascular infiltration with lymphocytes and plasma cells plus endothelial proliferation. This endarteritis results in occlusion of the blood supply leading to loss of epithelium and ulceration of the primary lesion of acquired syphilis, mucosal ulceration and the scaling of long-lasting papules in secondary syphilis, the necrosis and ulceration in gummatous syphilis and some of the tissue damage in cardiovascular and neurosyphilis. Tissue destruction is often more marked in late syphilis. The cellular infiltration accounts for the induration of the base of the primary lesion, the papule and the rubbery enlargement of lymph nodes in the secondary stage. This infiltration also provides much of the enlargement of late proliferative lesions. Healing is by fibrosis and scarring which leads to deformity and these are more marked in late syphilis.

Early acquired syphilis

Primary syphilis

Incubation period

This is usually 2–4 weeks.
The full range is 9–90 days.

Common presentation

This is a genital ulcer.

Clinical features

The treponeme probably cannot penetrate intact epithelium but can enter through any microscopic or macroscopic trauma such as may arise during sexual intercourse. Thus the primary lesion, or primary chancre as it is often called, tends to be found on the sites subject to trauma during intercourse. In the heterosexual male these are usually on the penis and include the:

coronal sulcus (Fig. 4.2),
glans,
meatus,
fraenum (Fig. 4.3),
prepuce (Fig. 4.4),
shaft (Fig. 4.5).
In the homosexual male the chancre may also be:
at or near the anus (Fig. 4.6),
in the anal canal, or rectum
where it is often asymptomatic.

In the female the primary chancre is usually on the vulva, especially the fourchette, or on the cervix. The vaginal wall is rarely involved. Genital chancres in women rarely cause symptoms.

In both sexes, but especially in homosexual males, chancres may occur at other sites. In homosexuals they are often situated on the lips.

In most cases the primary chancre is single. It begins as a dull red macule which soon become papular and ulcerates. The classical chancre is:

relatively painless,

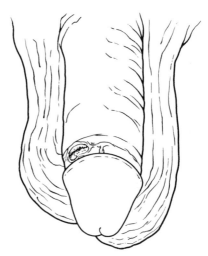

FIG. 4.2 Primary chancre on coronal sulcus. Note the classical chancre has the following features: round outline, well-defined margin, indurated (rubbery, thickened) base.
Compared to genital ulcers due to other causes it is relatively painless and non-tender and produces relatively more serum when traumatised.

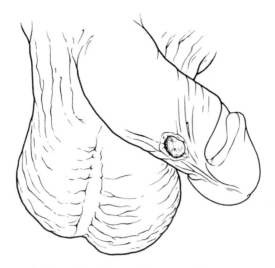

FIG. 4.3 Primary chancre on fraenum.

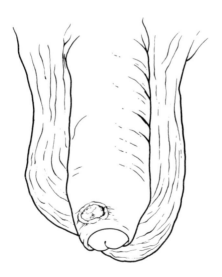

FIG. 4.4 Primary chancre on prepuce.

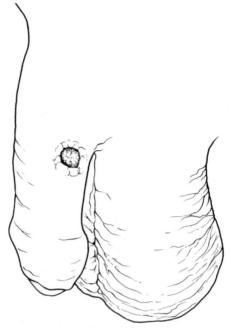

FIG. 4.5   Primary chancre on shaft.

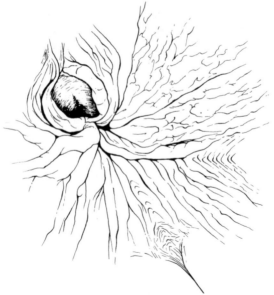

FIG. 4.6   Primary anal chancre.

relatively non-tender,

rounded,

has a well-defined margin,

an indurated rubbery base.

when traumatised it produces more serum than blood compared to genital ulcers due to other causes.

The base may be dull red or may be covered with a yellowish slough or a grey scab. While this sounds characteristic, the ulcers vary widely in appearance and any genital ulcer should be regarded as potentially syphilitic and investigated accordingly.

The regional lymph nodes are often involved; they are:

only moderately enlarged,

discrete,

rubbery in consistency,

painless,

non-tender.

If the ulcer becomes secondarily infected it may become painful and tender and the lymph nodes may also be painful, tender and develop a firmer consistency. There may be marked oedema of the surrounding tissues especially where the ulcer is under the prepuce, when phimosis may develop, or on the vulva. During pregnancy there may be greater swelling due to the greater vascularity and the ulcer may be larger. An anal chancre may resemble an anal fissure. Ulcers on the penis, vulva and anus are associated with inguinal adenopathy. Cervical and rectal lymphatic drainage is to the para-aortic lymph nodes.

Investigation

1. Unless antimicrobial therapy has already been started by someone else, efforts must always be made to identify *T. pallidum* by dark-ground microscopy as already described. If the first examination is negative, the patient should be instructed to:

bathe frequently with saline,

avoid sexual contact,

attend daily for at least two repeat examinations.

2. When the ulcer is in an inaccessible position, such as the rectum or on the cervix, it can be cleaned using bacteriological swabs (on orange sticks) and material for dark-ground microscopy can be collected using a bacteriological loop.

3. When conditions are optimal, *T. pallidum* can be recognised

within a minute of collecting the serum; a very satisfactory time for establishing firm diagnosis.

4. If the patient has been applying antiseptics and it is important to establish the diagnosis as soon as possible, then lymph node puncture may be undertaken if there is a reasonably large superficial node. To do this, clean the overlying skin with saline, hold the node firmly between the gloved finger and thumb, plunge a needle attached to a syringe firmly into the node, inject 0·1 ml sterile saline into the node, move the end of the needle gently around within the node, apply suction and withdraw. The fluid obtained is examined by the dark-ground method.

5. In addition, blood should always be taken for serological tests (VDRL, p. 47 and TPHA, p. 50).

Diagnosis

This depends on:
> an ulcer,
> identifying *T. pallidum*,
> positive results to serological tests (including at least one specific test) if *T. pallidum* cannot be identified, but efforts should always be made to find *T. pallidum*.

Treatment and management

Procaine penicillin 600,000 units daily for 10–12 days is the antimicrobial treatment of choice. In very large individuals increase the daily dose to 900,000 units.

In subjects who are known or suspected to be hypertensive to penicillin, give:
> oxytetracycline 2–3 g daily in divided doses for 14 or 15 days,
> *or*
> erythromycin in the same dosage.

Jarisch–Herxheimer reaction

Warn the patient that this reaction may develop a few hours after the start of therapy. There are two components:
1. General—with fever, tachycardia and the usual symptoms that accompany fever,

2. Local—with oedema and cellular infiltration of the chancre, and possible appearance of a widespread rash.

The general component lasts a few hours and has resolved by the following morning. The local component may take longer to resolve.

Tell the patient the symptoms are unpleasant but harmless and to retire to bed, take 2 aspirin tablets 4–6 hourly, and plenty of fluids.

The only local therapy needed is to keep the lesion clean with physiological saline.

The patient must abstain from intercourse until the ulcer has healed and the blood tests show a satisfactory response, namely the VDRL titre (see p. 48) starts to fall.

Cure rate

The penicillin regimen should give a cure rate of over 95 per cent and the oral preparations a slightly lower rate.

Follow-up after treatment

This is vital to ensure satisfactory cure. The patient should be seen:
 monthly for 3 months after starting treatment,
 3-monthly until a year after start of treatment,
 at 18 months,
 at 2 years after start of treatment (see Fig. 4.7).

Attendance

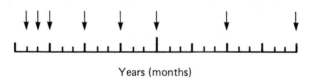

Years (months)

FIG. 4.7   Follow-up after treatment of primary and secondary syphilis.

At each visit:
 examine clinically,
 take blood for serological tests (VDRL and TPHA).

Relapse after treatment may be clinical or serological. Clinical relapse takes the form of an ulcer developing at the site of the original chancre; it is called monorecidive. Serological relapse is indicated by a secondary rise in the titre of the VDRL test after this has started to fall. In practice it is often difficult to distinguish between true relapse and re-infection.

Differential diagnosis

Conditions to be considered in patients presenting in temperate climates who have not recently visited the tropics:

herpes simplex (p. 167),
erosive balanitis (p. 212),
trauma (p. 218),
scabies (p. 188),
secondary syphilis,

and less commonly:

herpes zoster (p. 182),
carcinoma (p. 224),
Vincent's ulcers (p. 214),
orogenital ulceration, such as:
Stevens–Johnson syndrome (p. 227),
Behçet's syndrome (p. 225),
gumma (p. 54).

If the patient presents in a tropical climate or has recently returned from the tropics, consider the following:

chancroid (p. 195),
granuloma inguinale (p. 200),
lymphogranuloma venereum (p. 205),
tuberculosis (p. 228).

Course if untreated

If untreated, the primary lesion will heal in 3–6 weeks and may or may not leave a scar.

Some patients may then enter a latent phase; others start the secondary stage 3–6 weeks after the appearance of the primary chancre, so the secondary stage may develop while the chancre is still present.

Secondary acquired syphilis

Common presentation

The most common presentation is a rash.

Clinical features

It is in the secondary stage that the disease is obviously systemic. There is often a prodromal phase with non-specific features of systemic disease, such as:

malaise,
headache,
general aches and pains,
low-grade fever.

These symptoms may have such a gradual onset that the patient does not appreciate the illness until after treatment has started. These symptoms may be present for 1–3 weeks before the characteristic signs develop. These are:

rash	75% of patients,
lymphadenopathy	50% of patients,
mucosal ulceration	30% of patients,

and in 10 per cent or less of patients, involvement of:

viscera,
bones,
eyes,
central nervous system.

The rash starts as faint pink macules restricted to the trunk, where they may be denser on the sides of the abdomen, and on proximal parts of the limbs. These macules become papular and spread up to the face and down the limbs characteristically affecting the palms and soles. Later they became papulosquamous and the scabs may become so marked as to resemble psoriasis. Lesions are round in outline and dull red in colour. More lesions appear on flexor than on extensor surfaces and once the rash has reached the papular stage, different types of eruption are found on the same patient at the same time. The rash is usually non-irritant and is symmetrically distributed on both sides of the body. The rash may be most marked in the area covered by the underpants. Lesions in warm moist regions of the body, conditions which favour the treponeme, such as the perianal region, become large and are called condylomata lata

(Fig. 4.8). This type of papule is also favoured by the irritation of skin surfaces rubbing together and they may also occasionally occur in the vulva, in the axillae, under pendulous breasts, between the outer toes and on the lateral aspects of the scrotum. Occasionally, involvement of the scalp occurs causing the hair to fall out leaving a patchy alopecia. When papules are present for a long time they may develop an annular distribution.

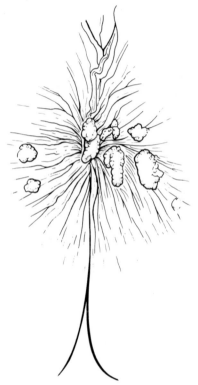

FIG. 4.8   Condylomata lata in secondary syphilis.

In some long-standing papules the scaling, due to endarteritis obliterans, becomes marked, specially in the middle of the papule, producing a core of scales and a lesion resembling a pustule—so called pustular syphilis. This may be more common in debilitated patients.

Skin lesions heal leaving faintly pigmented areas which gradually fade. The resulting depigmentation may be noticeable on the skin of the back of the neck, a condition known as the 'collar of Venus'.

Enlarged lymph nodes of secondary syphilis, like those of primary syphilis are:

    only moderately enlarged,
    discrete,
    rubbery,
    non-tender.

Enlarged nodes may be found in the regions shown in Figure 4.9, namely:

    posterior cervical chain, especially sub-occipital nodes,
    axillae,
    supracondylar region,
    inguinal region.

In fully-developed cases, nodes in all these regions may be involved, but in many cases only a few nodes in one or two sites may be affected.

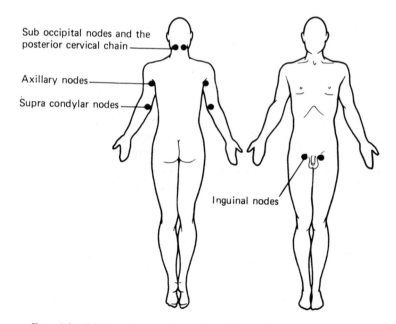

FIG. 4.9 Distribution of enlarged lymph nodes in secondary syphilis.

Mucosal ulcers initially are very superficial and difficult to see though outlined by a fine dull-red line. Later they become obvious with a greyish-white base edged with an obvious dull red, rounded margin. They are called mucous patches and may coalesce to form so-called snailtrack ulcers. Ulceration may affect the mucosa of the:
> genitals,
> mouth,
> pharynx,
> larynx.
Laryngeal involvement leads to hoarseness.

Involvement of the other systems is rare. Occasional hepatosplenomegaly may occur and secondary syphilitic hepatitis may be characterised by a disproportionately high alkaline phosphatase concentration. Bony involvement usually takes the form of osteoperiostosis, often with marked so-called osteoscopic pains, though other lesions may affect the locomotor system. Eye lesions are either anterior uveitis or choroidoretinitis. Central nervous system involvement usually takes the form of low-grade meningitis, with persistent headache which may be the presenting feature, and occasional cranial nerve lesions. The cerebrospinal fluid shows changes in some neurologically asymptomatic cases; this is called asymptomatic neurosyphilis, but the fluid is not routinely examined in secondary syphilis.

Investigation and diagnosis

The diagnosis should be strongly suspected from the clinical features in most cases of secondary syphilis, but it must be supported whenever possible by demonstrating *T. pallidum*. The organism can be found in serum obtained from papules and mucosal ulcers. Serum antibody tests are almost always positive in the secondary stage but should not be relied on to make a diagnosis. Always look for *T. pallidum* but note it cannot be demonstrated in the serum obtained from macules.

Treatment

Procaine penicillin 600,000 units daily for 14 or 15 days is the treatment of choice (again, in large individuals increase the daily dose to 900,000 units).

In subjects who are known or suspected to be hypersensitive to penicillin, give oxytetracycline or erythromycin 2–3 g daily in divided doses for 14 or 15 days.

The patient should be advised to abstain from intercourse until all the lesions have healed and the serological tests begin to show a satisfactory response. This takes about 3 months.

Cure rate

The penicillin regimen should give a cure rate of over 95 per cent and the oral preparations a slightly lower rate.

Follow-up after treatment

This is the same as for primary syphilis.

Relapse

As indicated, relapse is rare after the treatment outlined. Clinical or serological relapse may occur. Clinical relapse usually takes the form of lesions in the mouth, throat, at the anus, or on the skin. Serological relapse is indicated by a secondary rise in the VDRL test titre after a satisfactory fall. As in primary syphilis, it is often difficult to distinguish relapse from re-infection.

Differential diagnosis

This involves many conditions. The macular rash must be distinguished from:

> measles,
> rubella,
> drug rashes,
> pityriasis rosea,
> pityriasis versicolor (tinea versicolor),
> seborrhoeic dermatitis,
> erythema multiforme,

and, in certain tropical countries:

> rose spots of typhoid fever,
> leprosy.

The papular rash must be differentiated from:
    lichen planus,
    drug rashes,
    psoriasis,
    scabies,
    acne vulgaris,
    nodular leprosy.
Annular lesions may be mistaken for:
    fungal infections,
    impetigo,
    erythema multiforme.
Distinguish condylomata lata from:
    viral warts or condylomata accuminata (p. 174),
    anal tags.
Ulcers in the mouth or throat must be differentiated from:
    apthous ulcers,
    herpes labialis,
    acute tonsillitis,
    Vincent's angina,
    glandular fever,
    agranulocytosis,
    erythema multiforme or Stevens–Johnson syndrome (p. 227).
Secondary syphilitic lesions on the genital mucosa may resemble:
    herpes simplex (p. 167),
    lichen planus (p. 235),
    psoriasis (p. 233),
    circinate balanitis of Reiter's disease (p. 144).
and in women:
    the acute vulval ulcer of Behçet's syndrome (p. 225).
Lymphadenopathy may suggest:
    glandular fever,
    Hodgkin's disease,
    lymphoma.

Course if untreated

If untreated, the lesions heal over 2–3 months. Occasionally, there is a recurrence of secondary lesions within the first 2 years of infection. Such lesions are fewer and skin lesions are more nodular than in the first attack.

Usually, there is no such recurrence and the patient passes into the latent stage.

3-month follow-up for all patients

Details of the follow-up for other conditions are outlined in the relevant section. Note that as the maximum incubation period of syphilis is 90 days, ask *all* patients, with or without disease, to return 3 months after their first visit to ensure that syphilis is not missed. In addition see all patients with undiagnosed anogenital ulcers monthly for 3 months. At each of these visits:

examine clinically,
repeat serological tests.

CHAPTER 5

Antibody tests and latent syphilis

Antibody tests

Antibody tests are used to screen sera, hence the term serological tests, but antibodies may also be detected in cerebrospinal fluid.

Serum tests for syphilis antibodies are widely used in medicine to screen sera from:

women attending antenatal clinics,
blood donors each time they donate blood,
patients with cardiovascular disease,
patients with neurological disease,
patients with various dermatological and other conditions.

In STD clinics they are used to:

screen all patients for they have a high prevalence of treponemal disease,
establish the diagnosis of latent syphilis,
support clinical diagnosis of later forms of syphilis,
follow-up patients after treatment.

The tests can be divided into:

non-specific or lipoidal tests,
specific tests.

Non-specific or lipoidal tests

These tests are so called because a non-specific phospholipid antigen is used. The following tests are used:

Cardiolipin Wasserman reaction (CWR)

The first test described by Wasserman used a simple tissue extract.

ANTIBODY TESTS AND LATENT SYPHILIS 47

The active component was found to be the phospholipid, cardiolipin, which when mixed with lecithin and cholesterol became antigenic and was widely used. A complement fixation method is used; such procedures are cumbersome and flocculation tests have largely replaced them.

Kahn test

This was the first flocculation test, but has been superseded by other tests.

Venereal diseases reseach laboratory (VDRL) test

This simple flocculation test is cheap and easy to perform and has become a standard test used all over the world (Fig. 5.1). It becomes positive about 2 weeks after the appearance of the primary chancre. It can readily be done quantitatively.

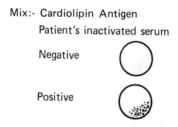

Mix:- Cardiolipin Antigen
Patient's inactivated serum

Negative

Positive

Inactivated by heating at 56 °C for 30 minutes

FIG. 5.1   The VDRL test.

Rapid plasma reagin (RPR) test

This is an even simpler version of the VDRL test and can be performed with minimal equipment.

Automated reagin test (ART)

As the name implies, this is an automated method for screening large numbers of sera.

These tests detect an antibody-like substance. It is not a specific antitreponemal antibody, but it appears more frequently and in higher titre in treponemal disease, especially venereal syphilis, than in any other condition. The behaviour of these tests is summarised in Figure 5.2. Positive results may be due to:

venereal syphilis,
other treponemal diseases,
false-positive results.

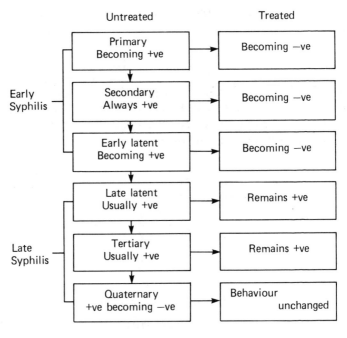

+ve: positive; —ve: negative

FIG. 5.2   VDRL serum antibody test in syphilis.

False-positive results

False-positive results to lipoidal tests may be due to:

technical or laboratory errors (common to all tests),
biological false-positive results,
Acute which may last for a maximum of 6 months, disappear spontaneously and may occur with almost any infection including:

viral pneumonia,
infectious mononucleosis,
chicken pox,
measles,
malaria.
and in association with pregnancy.

    Chronic lasting more than 6 months and commonly due to:

autoimmune diseases, especially systemic lupus erythematosis,
chronic infection such as tuberculosis,
other conditions, including:
    ageing,
    narcotic addiction,
    malignancy.

Specific tests

These were devised to overcome the problem caused by biological false-positive results to lipoidal tests. They use specific treponemal antigen but cannot differentiate between antibodies produced by the different treponemal diseases; this must be done on clinical grounds. The main specific antibody tests are as follows:

Reiter protein complement fixation test (RPCFT)

This test utilises the same complement fixation method as the CWR but with an antigen derived from the Reiter treponeme. The antigen is described as a group antigen for it is common to all treponemes, pathogen and saprophyte. The method has a number of disadvantages and has been replaced in many laboratories by the TPHA test (see below).

Fluorescent treponemal antibody-absorbed (FTA-ABS) test

The antigen used in this test is dead *T. pallidum* (Nichol's virulent strain) dried and fixed on a slide. Diluted patient's serum is added. If antibody is present it adheres to the treponemes. Antihuman antibody conjugated with fluorescein isothiocyanate is added which reacts with the patient's antibody (Fig. 5.3). The slide is then examined using a fluorescent microscope.

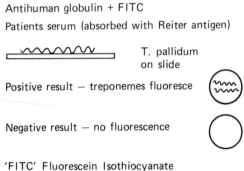

Antihuman globulin + FITC

Patients serum (absorbed with Reiter antigen)

T. pallidum
on slide

Positive result — treponemes fluoresce

Negative result — no fluorescence

'FITC' Fluorescein Isothiocyanate

FIG. 5.3   The FTA-ABS test.

This test can detect two antibodies. One is the treponemal group antibody detected by the RPCFT, common to all treponemes and present in low titre in many people's serum, probably in response to saprophytic treponemes. This can be removed by absorbing patients' sera with the antigen used for the RPCFT. Hence the term fluorescent treponemal antibody-*absorbed* test. This leaves antibody specific to *T. pallidum* and the allied treponemes pathogenic to man. This test is very specific and very sensitive, becoming positive around the time of appearance of the primary chancre. It is, however, somewhat cumbersome and a fluorescent microscope is needed.

Treponema pallidum haemagglutination (TPHA) test

In this test the antigen is a suspension of red cells coated with an ultrasonicate of *T. pallidum*. The patient's serum is diluted with a

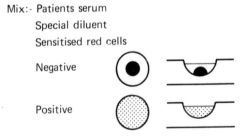

Mix:- Patients serum
Special diluent
Sensitised red cells

Negative

Positive

FIG. 5.4   Treponemal haemagglutination (TPHA) test.

special diluent which prevents non-specific reaction. The red cell suspension is then added; haemagglutination is easy to see (Fig. 5.4). The test is easy to perform and combines well in the laboratory with the VDRL test.

The TPHA test is as specific as the FTA-ABS test. When done by the original macro-method it is as sensitive at the beginning of an infection as the FTA-ABS; for reasons of economy a micro-method is often used and this gives a positive result later.

Treponema pallidum immobilisation (TPI) test

This was the first specific test and was described in 1949. In this test, a suspension of fresh live treponemes, complement, and patient's serum are mixed and examined microscopically; loss of motility indicates the presence of specific antitreponemal antibody. The test is highly specific but insensitive, taking longer to become positive in the course of an infection than any of the other methods. It is also

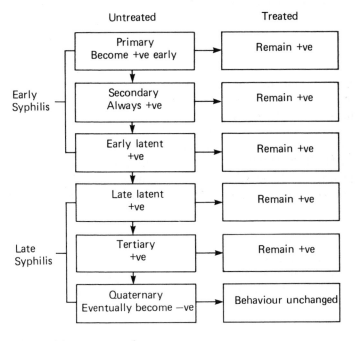

+ve: positive; −ve: negative

FIG. 5.5 Specific serum antibody tests in syphilis.

expensive and dangerous. It is regarded in the UK as the test against which others are assessed, though elsewhere the FTA-ABS test may serve this purpose.

The behaviour of the specific tests are summarised in Fig. 5.5.

In routine laboratories, the initial screening of samples is often done using the VDRL test alone. A positive result can then be checked with one of the specific tests and the VDRL test repeated quantitatively. A number of positive sera are missed this way and it is better, if facilities permit, to screen all sera with two tests such as the VDRL and TPHA tests.

Immunity

There is no relationship between circulating antibodies and immunity. Immunity develops slowly and declines slowly after adequate treatment. Much research currently concerns artificial immunisation but many difficulties must be overcome before a suitable vaccine will be available.

Latent syphilis

In early and late latent syphilis, there are no clinical signs and diagnosis may be suspected from the history but is based on results of serological tests. One sample is insufficient; a second sample should be taken one or two weeks after the first. One of the modern specific tests should be included such as the FTA-ABS or the TPHA tests. When a reference laboratory, such as the Venereal Diseases Reference Laboratory in London, is available the second sample should be sent there for verification. Once the second sample is known to have positive results:

X-ray the chest to exclude aortic calcification,

examine the cerebrospinal fluid.

Only if these investigations are negative is a diagnosis of latent treponemal disease correct. As already mentioned, differentiate venereal syphilis from other treponemal disease on clinical grounds.

Treatment

This comprises:

procaine penicillin, 600,000 units daily for 14–15 days,
when penicillin hypersensitivity is known or suspected, or
oxytetracycline or erythromycin 2–3 g in divided doses daily for
15 days.

Give prednisone 5 mg four times a day starting 24 hours before
the beginning of treatment, and continue for 24 hours after the
beginning to reduce the effects of the Jarisch–Herxheimer reaction.

Follow-up

The follow-up of latent syphilis is shown in Table 5.1.

TABLE 5.1   Follow-up of latent syphilis.

Initially, this is as in primary and secondary syphilis:
SEE:
    Monthly for 3 months,
    3-monthly for 9 months,
    6-monthly for 1 year,
    then once a year.
AT EACH VISIT:
    examine clinically,
    repeat serological tests.

Prognosis
Cure rates of 95 per cent or higher can be expected.

Complications
Serological relapse.

CHAPTER 6

Late acquired syphilis

Tertiary syphilis

If syphilis is not diagnosed and treated earlier, a patient may develop tertiary or benign gummatous syphilis 3–10 or more years after the primary stage. Tertiary syphilis is rare in the UK today but is still common elsewhere. Initially the tissues most commonly involved are:

> skin,
> mucous membranes,
> subcutaneous and submucous tissues,
> bones,
> occasionally joints.
> Ligaments are also involved.

Pathology

The characteristic lesion of this stage is the gumma. This:

> is usually localised,
> may be single or multiple,
> varies in diameter from 0·1 to several centimetres.

The exception is the diffuse gummatous reaction seen in the long bones. Histologically, the lesion is a granuloma with the detailed features already described.

Cutaneous gummas. These may be:

> nodular, occurring anywhere on the skin,
> squamous or psoriasiform, and found on the palms and soles.

They tend to heal leaving rounded, slightly depressed shiny scars.

Subcutaneous gummas usually occur on the lower leg and ulcerate (Fig. 6.1). The walls of the ulcers are vertical and the floor usually of clean granulation tissue. There may be necrotic yellowish white tissue forming a slough described as looking like 'wash leather'.

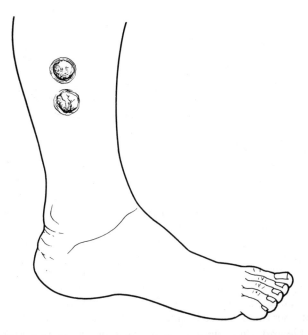

FIG. 6.1   Gummatous ulcers on lower leg in tertiary syphilis.

Mucosal gummas. These are usually localised and affect the submucous tissue of the:
mouth,
palate (Fig. 6.2),
larynx,
pharynx,
nasal septum.
They ulcerate producing a characteristic punched out appearance with a pale grey slough on the base, again described as looking like a 'wash leather'. Underlying bony structures may be destroyed.
Rarely, diffuse gummatous infiltration of the tongue occurs and is

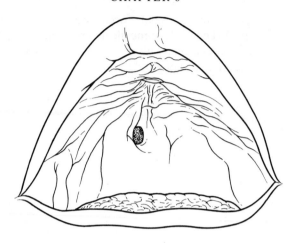

FIG. 6.2 Gummatous ulcer perforating hard palate in tertiary syphilis.

called 'chronic superficial glossitis'; a misleading term for this deep-seated inflammation.

Bony gummas. When these affect the long bones there is diffuse gummatous subperiosteal reaction which especially affects the anterior margin of the tibia. There is new bone formation. The main symptom is deep-seated boring pain. Irregular tender lumps may be palpable and when there is much new bone on the anterior margin of the tibia, it may become rounded giving the appearance of a sabre: 'sabre tibia' (Fig. 6.3).

The skull may be affected but here localised lytic lesions appear. Again, the main sympton is pain.

Diagnosis

The diagnosis rests on:
    history,
    clinical findings,
    result of serological tests,
    radiographs,
    biopsy, if necessary.

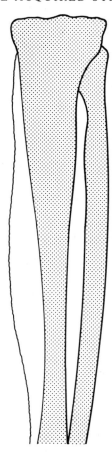

FIG. 6.3 Radiographic appearance of gummatous osteoperiostosis of anterior margin of tibia (sabre tibia) in tertiary syphilis.

Treatment

The treatment of first choice is:
  procaine penicillin 600,000 units daily for 15 days.
 Otherwise use:
  oxytetracycline or erythromycin 2–3 g daily in divided doses for
    15 days.
Again, give prednisone 5 mg four times a day starting 24 hours before the beginning of treatment and continue for a further 24 hours to reduce the effects of the Jarisch–Herxheimer reaction.

Cure rates are 90–95 per cent, being higher with penicillin than with oral preparations.

Follow-up

As in Figure 6.4.

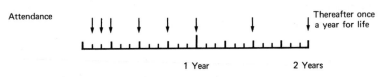

Attendance

Thereafter once a year for life

1 Year 2 Years

At each visit: examine clinically, repeat blood tests

FIG. 6.4   Follow-up after treatment of late syphilis.

Differential diagnosis

Differentiate proliferative skin lesions from:
    psoriasis,
    seborrhoeic dermatitis,
    mycoses,
    dermatophytoses,
    cutaneous lesions of reticulosis,
and chronic infections such as:
    tuberculosis,
    leprosy.
  Ulcerative cutaneous gummas must be distinguished from:
    rodent ulcers on the face,
    varicose ulcers on the legs,
    squamous epithelioma.
  Tertiary syphilis of bone must be distinguished from:
    osteomyelitis,
    Paget's disease,
    myelomatosis.

Cardiovascular syphilis

Cardiovascular syphilis may appear in about 10 per cent of untreated syphilitic patients after a latent period of 10 or 20 or more years.

Men are affected more than women,

Negroes are affected more than whites.

In general, patients with cardiovascular syphilis should be managed in consultation with a cardiologist. The more specialised cardiac aspects are only outlined here.

Ascending aortitis

T. pallidum invades the vasa vasorum at the root of the aorta leading to endarteritis and periarteritis with the histological changes seen in other forms of syphilis. These in turn lead to loss of elastic tissue and dilatation, and fibrosis with shrinkage and deformity.

Uncomplicated ascending aortitis cannot be detected clinically or radiologically. Once calcification develops changes may be seen on a plain chest radiograph. This in itself does not usually affect life expectancy.

Echocardiography shows early uncomplicated dilatation of the ascending aorta, but remember this may have other causes.

Aortitis may be complicated (see Fig. 6.5) by:

    coronary ostial stenosis leading to symptoms of coronary insufficiency,

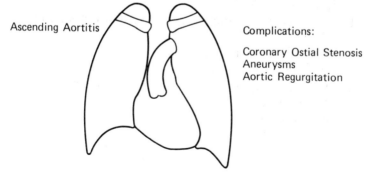

Ascending Aortitis

Complications:

Coronary Ostial Stenosis
Aneurysms
Aortic Regurgitation

FIG. 6.5 Ascending aortitis and its complications in cardiovascular syphilis.

aneurysm which presents in various ways according to the site involved,

aortic regurgitation, often symptomatic but may present in various ways.

The diagnosis of cardiovascular syphilis is outlined in Table 6.1. Patients with cardiovascular syphilis may also have neurosyphilis. All cases should have a lumbar puncture.

TABLE 6.1   Diagnosis.

DIAGNOSIS OF SYPHILIS DEPENDS AS USUAL ON
   History,
   Symptoms,
   Signs,
   Serological tests.

DIAGNOSIS OF CARDIOVASCULAR SYPHILIS DEPENDS ON
   Clinical features,
   Serological results:
     VDRL test usually positive,
     TPHA ⎤ results nearly always positive,
     FTA (ABS) ⎦
   Results of special investigations.

Coronary ostial stenosis (Fig. 6.6)

This is now rare in Britain. Stenosis leads to:
   angina,
   myocardial infarction.

FIG. 6.6 Coronary ostial stenosis in cardiovascular syphilis. Also shows widening of aortic valve ring.

Presentation and clinical features

Pain is usually the presenting symptom. While the clinical features of angina and myocardial infarction due to coronary ostial stenosis resemble those due to coronary atheroma, note that the anginal pain may be atypical radiating as high as the lower jaw and as low as the epigastrium. Syphilitic aortic regurgitation and aneurysm may also be present.

Investigation and diagnosis

The diagnosis will depend on the:
    clinical features,
    results of serological tests (Table 6.1).
   Special investigations which may show the changes listed in Table 6.2.

TABLE 6.2   Special investigations in coronary ostial stenosis.

Investigation	Finding
Echocardiography	Dilatation of the aortic root,
Chest radiograph	Calcification of the ascending aorta,
Electrocardiograph (ECG)	Changes of ischaemia.
Aortography and coronary angiography	Coronary ostial stenosis (as distinct from the much more common coronary atheroma).

Treatment

Treatment of all forms of cardiovascular syphilis includes:
    modification of the patients' way of life,
    antitreponemal therapy, i.e. antimicrobials,
    other measures, such as surgery.

The patients' way of life. In most forms of cardiovascular syphilis it is important that patients modify their way of life for undue activity worsens the prognosis. Anginal pain limits the patients' activities. After a myocardial infarct, especially if the obstruction has been surgically removed from the coronary ostia, it is important that patients gradually resume a reasonable level of activity and take regular daily exercise compatible with their level of recovery. Excess weight and smoking must be curbed. Discuss the patients' sexual activities; many patients are too shy to ask about it. The patients' jobs may need consideration if they are energetic; so may their housing if they live in a top-floor flat. But, remember people are happiest doing familiar tasks in familiar surroundings.

Remember the two axioms when managing these patients:
'moderation in all things', and
'a little of what you fancy does you good'.

Antitreponemal therapy. Antimicrobials must be given to arrest the syphilitic inflammatory process.

Disease may still progress because of the destruction of elastic tissue leading to dilatation, aneurysms or aortic regurgitation; fibrosis may lead to contraction and deformity of valve cusps and coronary ostia.

Admit the patient for observation at the beginning of treatment.
Doses:
procaine penicillin 600,000 units daily for 15–21 days,
or, in penicillin hypersensitive patients:
oxytetracycline or erythromycin, 2–3 g daily in divided doses for 21–28 days.
In large patients, give procaine penicillin 900,000 units daily.

If possible, delay surgery for 3 months after antimicrobials to allow fibrosis to replace inflammatory tissue.

Take care at the start of antimicrobial therapy because the Jarisch–Herxheimer reaction can have serious effects. The fever and tachycardia of the general component can lead to left ventricular failure while local oedema and cellular infiltration can exacerbate coronary ostial stenosis. These may be suppressed, but not prevented, by giving prednisone 30 mg daily in divided doses starting 24–48 hours before starting antimicrobials. Continue the full dose for 24–48 hours after the start and then reduce by 5 mg per day. Observe the patient closely for 24 hours after the first injection in consultation with a cardiologist. Admit the patient to a coronary care ward, if available; if not, admit the patient and monitor the ECG.

Treat syphilitic angina in the same way as angina due to atheroma. Myocardial infarction should also be treated in the same way as infarction due to atheroma.

(1) treat myocardial infarction medically,

(2) allow recovery,
(3) treat with penicillin.

Operation. Relief of the coronary ostial stenosis should be undertaken where possible. Operation must be preceded by accurate demonstration of the stenosis by aortography and coronary angiography.

Prognosis of coronary ostial stenosis

Prognosis of angina is:
    fair until other symptoms develop,
    poor once signs develop.

Prognosis after infarction is on the whole worse than the prognosis after infarction due to coronary atheroma.

Follow-up

See the patient at intervals outlined in Figure 6.4. Visits should if possible, coincide with appointments to see the cardiologist who must also follow the patient. At each visit:
    examine clinically,
    repeat serological tests,
    repeat special investigations in consultation with the cardiologist.

Complications

Sudden death is the main complication which may occur without warning, or following a myocardial infarct.

Aortic regurgitation or aneurysm may develop.

Left ventricular failure may complicate coronary ostial stenosis alone but is more likely when there is also aortic regurgitation.

Differential diagnosis

Differentiate coronary ostial stenosis from coronary atheroma. This will require aortography and coronary angiography.

Aortic regurgitation

Initially, this is due to widening of the aortic ring associated with dilatation of the ascending aorta. Later there is deformity of the valve cusps with increased regurgitation.

Clinical features

Aortic regurgitation can remain symptomless for long periods. When symptoms develop, they are the same as those of aortic regurgitation due to any cause and include:

    breathlessness,

    palpitations,

    angina in severe cases.

The signs are those of aortic regurgitation due to any cause and include:

    high amplitude collapsing pulse,

    displaced apex with sustained left ventricular heave,

    high pitched blowing early diastolic murmur usually louder down the left sternal edge, but sometimes louder down the right sternal edge,

    associated systolic murmur at the base ('to and fro' murmur),

    low-pitched rumbling mid-diastolic murmur at apex in severe cases (Austin Flint murmur),

    signs of left ventricular failure.

Investigations and diagnosis

The diagnosis rests on:

    clinical features and results of serological tests (Table 6.1),

    investigations which may show results listed in Table 6.3.

Treatment

Way of life. Patients with only minor regurgitation need not modify their life at all. As features develop and worsen the patients gradually have to reduce their activities. Once left ventricular failure develops, then restriction down to sedentary life becomes necessary.

Antitreponemal therapy. Antimicrobials as already outlined.

TABLE 6.3   Special investigations in aortic regurgitation.

Investigation	Finding
Echocardiography	Aortic dilatation, Volume load on left ventricle, Associated mitral valve changes.
Chest radiograph	Aortic calcification, Left ventricular enlargement.
ECG	Signs of left ventricular hypertrophy ST and T wave changes which may be due to coincidental coronary ostial stenosis.

Left ventricular failure. Usual measures (see page 71).

Surgery. Consider valve replacement in some cases with:
   marked regurgitation,
   left ventricular failure.
Consult a surgeon early, but if possible wait 3 months after the start of antimicrobials before operation.

Prognosis
Asymptomatic patients with small leaks can remain symptomless for long periods after completing antitreponemal therapy.
   Women do better than men.
   As in aortic regurgitation due to other causes, symptoms rapidly worsen once the heart enlarges above a certain size.

Follow-up

This is as in coronary ostial stenosis. In addition the cardiologist must follow the patient carefully and arrange repeated ECGs and echocardiographs to judge the time for aortic valve replacement.

Complications

Sub-acute bacterial endocarditis is rare.

Coronary ostial stenosis and aneurysms may develop.

Left ventricular failure, which is more likely to occur when there is also coronary ostial stenosis.

Differential diagnosis

This is summarised in Table 6.4.

TABLE 6.4   Differential diagnosis of syphilitic aortic regurgitation.

Rheumatic heart disease,
Congenital bicuspid aortic valve,
Atherosclerotic aortic valve disease and hypertension.

OCCASIONALLY
   Reiter's disease,
   Ankylosing spondylitis,
   Marfan's syndrome.

RARELY
   Other conditions.

Aneurysm

While the classical site for a syphilitic aneurysm is the ascending aorta (Fig. 6.7), syphilis also causes aneurysms of the aortic arch and descending thoracic aorta. Syphilis is rarely responsible for aneurysms of the abdominal aorta, especially distal to the renal arteries. Aneurysms may be fusiform or saccular.

Saccular aneurysms of the thoracic aorta are usually due to syphilis. In areas of the world where late syphilis is now uncommon, fusiform aneurysms, especially of the descending aorta, are usually due to atheroma.

ANEURYSM OF THE ASCENDING AORTA
('ANEURYSM OF SIGNS')

These aneurysms bulge forward against the anterior chest wall and into the right lung.

Presentation and clinical features

Pain is the common presenting symptoms. Signs include:
   expansile pulsation in 2nd and 3rd right interspaces,
   dullness to percussion in 2nd and 3rd right interspaces,

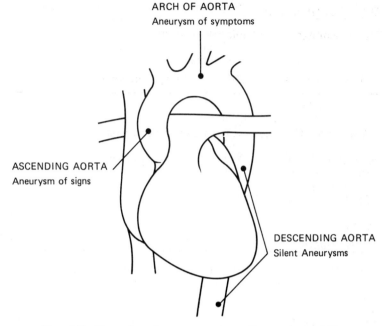

FIG. 6.7 Sites of aortic aneurysms in cardiovascular syphilis.

    loud systolic murmur,
    loud 2nd aortic sound,
    and signs of aortic regurgitation.

Diagnosis

This rests on:
    clinical features and results of serological tests (Table 6.1),
    investigations which may show results listed in Table 6.5.

ANEURYSM OF THE AORTIC ARCH ('ANEURYSM OF SYMPTOMS')

This aneurysm usually arises from the convex surface of the arch of the aorta.

TABLE 6.5 Special investigations for aneurysms of ascending aorta.

Plain radiographs	May show aneurysms, Left ventricular enlargement.
Echocardiograph	Shows diameter at level of aortic ring,
ECG	Shows no change for aneurysm alone, if left ventricular enlargement due to aortic regurgitation, features in Table 6.3 will appear.
Cardiac catheterisation/ angiography	If surgery contemplated.
Computerised axial tomography (where available)	Shows diameter of aneurysm above aortic ring.

Clinical features

As indicated above, these aneurysms can produce a wide variety of symptoms which are summarised in Table 6.6.

Investigations and diagnosis

These depend on:
        clinical features and results of serologicl tests (Table 6.1),
        results of special investigations, namely:
                plain chest radiographs which may show a large aneurysm,
                barium swallow which show a smaller aneurysm,

TABLE 6.6 Summary of symptoms of aneurysm of aortic arch. Gradual enlargement of the aneurysm has the following effects.

Effect	Clinical feature
Pressure on trachea	Stridor, 'brassy cough'
Stretching left recurrent laryngeal nerve	Hoarseness.
Pressure on sympathetic chain	Ptosis, meiosis, enophthalmos (Horner's syndrome).
Pressure on left main bronchus	Atelectasis, tracheal tug.
Pressure on superior vena cava	Obstruction.

angiography which is indicated if surgery is being considered and may be necessary to differentiate from aortic dissection.

ANEURYSM OF DESCENDING THORACIC AORTA ('ANEURYSM WITHOUT SYMPTOMS AND SIGNS')

This type of syphilitic aneurysm is rare.

Clinical features

Usually there are no symptoms. The occasional patient with an enlarging aneurysm complains of continuous boring backache due to pressure on the bodies of the 7th to 11th thoracic vertebrae.

Investigations and diagnosis

As indicated in Table 6.1, the diagnosis of syphilis depends on the clinical features and results of serological tests. An aneurysm of the descending thoracic aorta should be suspected from the characteristic pain.

Special investigations include:
   plain radiographs of the dorsal spine which may show erosion of the vertebral bodies,
   computerised axial tomography (where available) to show the diameter of the aneurysm,
   angiography if surgery is considered.

Treatment of aortic aneurysms

Way of life. A sedentary way of life is indicated.

Antimicrobial therapy is as already outlined for coronary ostial stenosis.

Surgery. Consult a surgeon early. If possible wait 3 months after the start of antimicrobials before operation. Saccular aneurysms not involving branches of the aorta can be replaced by an orlon graft.

Prognosis

On the whole this is bad for sudden death may occur at any time.

The operative mortality for aneurysms varies from about 5 to 15 per cent but postoperative survival is good.

Complications

The main complications of all aneurysms is rupture leading to death.

Aneurysm of ascending aorta

Rupture may be into the:
   pericardial sac producing tamponade,
   pleural space producing haemothorax and pulmonary collapse,
   right bronchus or lung producing torrential haemoptysis,
   and anteriorily through the chest wall producing torrential haemorrhage.

Aneurysm of the arch

This may rupture into the:
   trachea or a bronchus as above,
   oesophagus producing dramatic haematemesis,
   mediastinum producing pressure symptoms,
   superior vena cava producing symptoms of cardiac failure.

Aneurysms of the descending thoracic aorta

These rarely rupture.

Differential diagnosis

This is summarised in Table 6.7.

ANEURYSMS OF OTHER VESSELS

Syphilis should be considered in the differential diagnosis of any aneurysm.

TABLE 6.7 Differential diagnosis of aortic aneurysms.

MEDIASTINAL MASSES DUE TO:
Neoplasms, e.g. thymic, bronchial,
Enlarged lymph nodes,
Cysts (dermoid, lymphatic),
Oesophageal obstruction,
Intrathoracic goitre.
FUSIFORM ANEURYSMS MAY BE DUE TO:
Atheroma,
Trauma (deceleration injuries).
AND OCCASIONALLY:
Idiopathic aortic arch syndrome,
Marfan's syndrome.

Left ventricular failure

Aetiology

This is due to:
aortic regurgitation,
coronary ostial stenosis, particuarly when it is complicated by
myocardial infarction,
Note that myocardial ischaemia due to coronary atheroma may also
be present.

Clinical features and diagnosis

The clinical features and hence diagnosis are the same as the
features of left ventricular failure due to any other cause. In
addition, other features of syphilis may be present.

Treatment

1. *First* treat left ventricular failure with conventional
   measures,
2. wait till the cardiac condition has stabilised,
3. *then*, if the patient has not had antitreponemal therapy give
   antimicrobials as outlined for coronary ostial stenosis,
4. observe the patient carefully at the start of therapy in case
   there is a Jarisch–Herxheimer reaction; if this occurs
   intensify therapy for cardiac failure.

Prognosis

Once left ventricular failure has developed, the prognosis for the underlying condition, especially aortic regurgitation, is worse.

Differential diagnosis

Left ventricular failure due to cardiovascular syphilis must be differentiated from left ventricular failure due to the causes listed in Table 6.4. In addition, consider:

> myocardial ischaemia,
> cardiac arrhythmias,
> sub-acute bacterial endocarditis.

Neurosyphilis

This may appear in about 10 per cent of untreated syphilitic patients after a period of 10 and often 30 or more years. It is more common in men than in women, but the incidence has declined markedly in most western countries in recent years.

Classification is difficult because of overlap of clinical manifestations, but the following is based on the main clinical and pathological involvement:

> asymptomatic neurosyphilis,
> meningovascular syphilis,
> parenchymatous neurosyphilis:
>> affecting the brain: general paralysis of the insane (GPI)
>> affecting the spinal cord: tabes dorsalis.

Examination of the cerebrospinal fluid *must* be performed in all cases in which neurosyphilis is suspected and should be done in all cases of:

> latent treponemal disease,
> cardiovascular syphilis,
> tertiary syphilis.

The examination of the cerebrospinal fluid is summarised in Table 6.8.

In general, patients with neurosyphilis should be managed in consultation with a neurologist or where appropriate, a psychiatrist,

TABLE 6.8 Examination of the cerebrospinal fluid should include the following.

White cell count,
Total protein concentration,
IgG concentration or Lange colloidal gold curve,
Antibodies as detected by the VDRL and TPHA tests.

ophthalmologist or otologist. This chapter concentrates on the syphilitic aspects.

Asymptomatic neurosyphilis

This is the diagnosis in patients with no clinical abnormality, confirmed positive results to serum antibody tests and abnormal cerebrospinal fluid. Unless adequate treatment is given clinical neurosyphilis may develop, in particular if all four parameters of the cerebrospinal fluid are abnormal the patient will probably develop GPI.

Treatment

Treatment consists of antitreponemal antimicrobials. Give:
    procaine penicillin 900,000 units i.m. daily for 21 days,
    or in penicillin hypersensitive patients:
    oxytetracycline or erythromycin 2–3 g daily in divided doses for
    21–28 days.
In large patients give procaine penicillin 1·2 megaunits daily.

As in cardiovascular syphilis, the Jarisch–Herxheimer reaction may cause problems. Observe the patient in hospital for 24 hours after the first dose of antimicrobial. The Jarisch–Herxheimer reaction may be suppressed but not prevented by prednisone: give 30 mg prednisone in divided doses daily, starting 24–48 hours before the first dose, continue for 24–48 hours after the first dose and then reduce by 5 mg per day.

Follow-up

See Figure 6.4 for when patients should be seen.
    At each visit:
    examine clinically,
    repeat serological tests,
    after 3–6 months, repeat lumbar puncture.

Ensure that the white cell count returns to normal, which it usually does after 3 months. Total protein usually returns to normal after 6 months, but in a few cases remains raised. The VDRL titre should fall, but it and the specific antibody tests often remain positive. Further treatment must be given if the white cell count is still raised 6 months after treatment. If the protein is still raised but the patient is clinically satisfactory and serum antibody tests are satisfactory, then further treatment is not indicated. If serum VDRL titres start to rise or neurological features develop, the lumbar puncture must be repeated.

Meningovascular syphilis

Because the meninges and vessels are so closely related they are often affected together. For simplicity they are considered separately. Predominantly meningeal disease affecting the brain produces features of low grade meningitis with:

insidious onset,
headache (rarely, nausea and vomiting),
irritability,
cranial nerve palsies (especially III and VI),
pupillary abnormalities,
papilloedema,
(late progression to hydrocephalus).

When the spinal cord is mainly affected there are features of meningomyelitis with:

upper motor neurone features in the lower limbs,
lower motor neurone features in the upper limbs.

Disease predominantly affecting the cerebral arteries shows the same clinical syndromes as in degenerative cerebrovascular disease, especially:

hemiplegia,
hemisensory defect,
dysphasia,
hemianopia.

Where the spinal arteries are affected, it is the larger anterior spinal arteries that are important compared to the small posterior arteries which can be occluded without overt disease. Clinical features of anterior spinal artery occlusion are those of spinal transection with:

initial flaccid paralysis,
later spastic paraplegia.

TABLE 6.9   Results of investigations in meningovascular syphilis.

Serum lipoidal (VDRL) tests usually positive,
Serum specific tests (TPHA) almost always positive,
CSF usually abnormal with changes in three of the:
    White cell count,
    Total protein,
    IgG or Lange curve,
    Antibody tests,
but not in all four parameters.

There is a sensory level.

Serum antibody and cerebrospinal fluid findings are summarised in Table 6.9.

Treatment

Give antimicrobials as outlined under asymptomatic neurosyphilis.

Manage paraplegia in the usual way.

Follow-up

Follow-up as outlined for asymptomatic neurosyphilis on page 73 and Figure 6.4.

Prognosis

The prognosis is usually good, the patient returning to a full and normal life.

Differential diagnosis

This is summarised in Table 6.10.

General paralysis of the insane (GPI)

This condition affects the cerebral cortex (Fig. 6.8). Onset is usually between 45 and 55 years and is insidious with:
    loss of concentration,
        memory,
        judgment,

carelessness in appearance,
        behaviour.
Occasionally, the onset is sudden with:
    an acute confusional state,
    convulsion.
Later frank dementia develops often with delusions of grandeur but
these are related to the patient's background and may not appear
grand at first sight. On examination:

TABLE 6.10 Differential   diagnosis   of   meningovascular
                            neurosyphilis.

Syphilitic Meningitis	Tuberculous meningitis.
	Meningococcal meningitis,
	Aseptic meningitis,
	Brain abscess,
	Brain tumour,
	Other space occupying lesions.
Meningomyelitis	Motor neurone disease,
	Multiple sclerosis,
	Spinal tumour,
	Cervical spondylosis.
	Cerebral atheroma.
Syphilitic cerebrovascular disease	Cerebral atheroma.
Syphilitic spino-vascular disease	Spinal tumour,
	Transverse myelitis,
	Spinal transection.

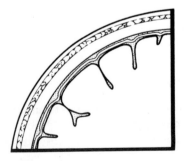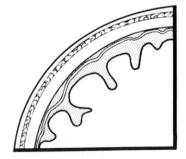

FIG. 6.8   Cortical atrophy in GPI.

upper motor neurone signs are present in lower limbs,
tremor may be present in fingers,
minor pupillary changes are common,
Argyll Robertson type of pupillary changes suggest an element
    of tabes (taboparesis).
There are no sensory changes in GPI as opposed to tabes dorsalis.
The results of investigations are summarised in Table 6.11.

TABLE 6.11   Results of investigations in untreated GPI.

Serum VDRL and TPHA tests positive.
Cerebrospinal fluid:
    Raised white cells,
    Raised total protein,
    Raised IgG or abnormal Lange curve,
    Antibodies (VDRL and TPHA).

In the late stages dementia becomes marked as does the spastic
paraparesis and the patient becomes bedridden and incontinent.
Death may be due to convulsions or intercurrent respiratory or
urinary tract infection.

Treatment

Antimicrobials as outlined for asymptomatic neurosyphilis. Obtain
the help of a psychiatrist.

Follow-up

As outlined for asymptomatic neurosyphilis on page 73 and Figure
6.4.

Prognosis

On the whole, prognosis is good. The labourer normally returns to
his previous work. The skilled tradesman or executive probably
occupies a lower grade than before. Some cases deteriorate so after
15 or 20 years they may be so demented that they require
institutional care.

Differential diagnosis

This is summarised in Table 6.12.

TABLE 6.12   Differentiate GPI from:

Psychotic manifestations	Cerebral arteriosclerosis, Manic depressive psychosis, Schizophrenia, Alcoholism, Drug side-effects, Pre-senile dementia, Senile dementia, Cerebral tumours, Other cerebral space-occupying lesions.
Paraparesis	Disseminated sclerosis, Vitamin B_{12} neuropathy.

Tabes dorsalis

This condition affects the posterior columns of the spinal cord. The clinical features of this form of neurosyphilis often take longer to appear than any others. The patient may present complaining of:

    falling over in the dark,

    difficulty in walking,

    shooting (lightning) pains in the legs.

Other symptoms include paraesthesiae (a feeling of walking on cottonwool, or pins and needles around the waist), bladder and bowel disturbance, impotence, and visual impairment. Signs include:

    ataxic tabetic gait: wide based and high stepping with visual compensation, worse in dark and when descending stairs.

    pupillary changes:

        classical Argyll Robertson pupils are:

            small,

            unequal,

            irregular.

They:

    fail to react to light,

    do react to accommodation.

These classical changes are now rare and any change may occur.

Loss of:

    proprioception,
    deep pain in Achilles tendon and perhaps testes,
    superficial pain and touch over:
        nose,
        sternum,
        ulnar border of arms,
        peroneal border of legs,
        perineal region (see Fig. 6.9),
    loss of tone and deep reflexes,
    optic atrophy,
    bladder disturbance (atonia and loss of sensation),
    trophic ulcers and trophic degeneration of joints (Charcot's
        joints).

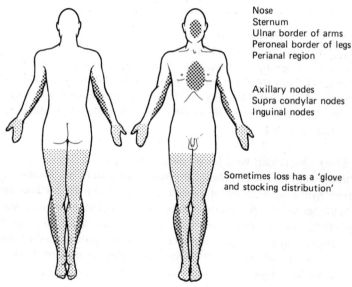

Nose
Sternum
Ulnar border of arms
Peroneal border of legs
Perianal region

Axillary nodes
Supra condylar nodes
Inguinal nodes

Sometimes loss has a 'glove
and stocking distribution'

FIG. 6.9　Distribution of superficial sensory loss in tabes dorsalis.

In addition, there may be:
    visceral crises including abdominal pain resembling perforated
        peptic ulcer or renal colic.
Results of investigations are summarised in Table 6.13.

TABLE 6.13   Results of investigations
in tabes dorsalis.

SERUM
  VDRL
    Positive in about 70% of cases,
    Negative in about 30% of cases.
  TPHA
    Usually positive,
    Occasionally negative.
CSF
  Usually changes in two or three of:
    Cell count,
    Total protein,
    IgG or Lange curve,
    Antibody tests (VDRL and TPHA).

Treatment

Antimicrobials as outlined.

Control lighting pains and paraesthesiae with analgesics. Strong analgesics in younger patients can lead to problems with addiction. Vitamin B_{12}, phenytoin, carbamazepine and corticosteroids have all been tried but none are of proven value. Optic atrophy with visual impairment may be improved with corticosteroids but these too are unproven.

Bladder atonia can best be managed by regular micturition with manual compression to help emptying. This may be assisted by a parasympathetic stimulator such as carbachol 0·25 mg injected subcutaneously. A grossly distended bladder may need catheterisation at first though this should be avoided if possible. If the above measures are unsuccessful a permanent indwelling catheter may be required. Urinary infection should be treated according to results of urine cultures; sterility may be maintained by giving methenamine mandelate.

Trophic ulcers. Prevention is the best measure. Advise about sensible shoes and socks. Ulcers need careful cleaning, dressing, rest and antimicrobials.

Trophic joints once disorganised and unstable need external support with splinting (Fig. 6.10).

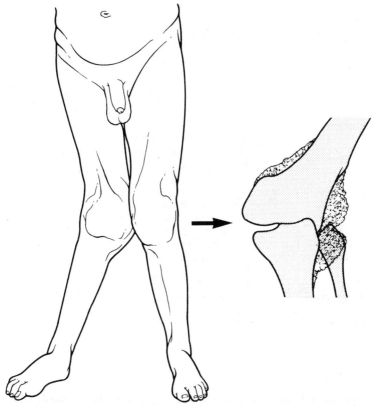

FIG. 6.10 Trophic joint in neurosyphilis. Destructive arthropathy due to sensory loss in tabes dorsalis (Charcot joint).

Visceral crises. The main problem is recognition. Treat with rest and analgesics.

Follow-up.

This is as already outlined for asymptomatic neurosyphilis on page 73 and Figure 6.4.

Prognosis

Prognosis is bad. While the inflammatory process is arrested, symptoms continue.

Differential diagnosis

This is summarised in Table 6.14.

TABLE 6.14   Differential diagnosis of tabes dorsalis.

Peripheral neuropathy	Alcoholism,
	Nutritional deficiencies,
	Diabetic neuropathy,
	Infective polyneuritis,
	Lead neuropathy.
Posterior column signs	Multiple sclerosis,
	Vitamin B_{12} neuropathy,
	Carcinomatous neuropathy,
	Friedrich's ataxia.
Bladder distention	Prostatic hypertrophy.
Trophic joints	Syringomyelia,
	Osteoarthritis,
	Prolonged intra-articular steroids.
Visceral crises	Perforated peptic ulcer,
	Renal colic

Gummas

Gummas of brain and spinal cord are very rare. They usually arise from the meninges. They may be single or multiple. They cause symptoms and signs of space occupying lesions. Manage these patients in consultation with a neurologist.

In the serum, lipoidal antigen (VDRL) tests are usually positive and the specific tests (TPHA) are positive.

Cerebrospinal fluid pressure may be raised. Several, but not all parameters are abnormal.

Diagnosis is often made by biopsy because of the presentation with features of a space occupying lesion.

Treatment

procaine penicillin 0·9–1·2 megaunits daily, for 15–21 days, *or* erythromycin or oxytetracycline 2–3 g daily in divided doses for 21–28 days.

Follow-up

As already outlined for asymptomatic neurosyphilis on page 73, Figure 6.4.

Prognosis

Good.
   Differentiate from other space occupying lesions.

CHAPTER 7

Congenital syphilis

Transmission of infection

Congenital syphilis is transmitted by the mother to the fetus *in utero*. While in general syphilis is only infectious during the first 2 years of life, transmission to the fetus may be an exception and a mother may infect her fetus occasionally 4, and exceptionally 6, years after acquiring syphilis.

T. pallidum probably crosses the placenta after the fourth month of pregnancy. If it crosses earlier disease does not follow. Syphilis is not a cause of abortion during the first 4 months of pregnancy.

Maternal history

In general, children born earlier in a family have more severe congenital syphilis than those born later, but there are many exceptions. A congenital syphilitic baby does not infect its mother who has natural immunity.

Prevention

Congenital syphilis can be prevented theoretically by serologically testing all pregnant women. However, the woman may be incubating the disease when tested, or may acquire it afterwards, while even in highly developed countries a few women avoid ante-natal care.

Treatment of the infected mother during the first 16 weeks of pregnancy prevents congenital syphilis. Treatment, even late in pregnancy, with procaine penicillin 600,000 units daily for 10–15 days arrests infection in the fetus.

Prevalence

Prevalence is low in Britain with about 100–200 cases annually. In contrast, in some tropical countries congenital syphilis contributes significantly to fetal and infant mortality.

Pathology

The placenta has been described as bulky, heavy, pale and greasy. In fact, the placenta may look macroscopically normal, though there may be histological changes. There are few treponemes.

Once the treponemes enter the fetal circulation they immediately spread throughout the fetus. They provoke the same histological reaction as in the adult, the characteristic features being an arteritis with a round cell and plasma cell infiltration.

The fetus may be overwhelmed by the infection and die when it will be expelled. The dead syphilitic fetus (Fig. 7.1) has a:
>   macerated appearance,
>   collapsed skull,
>   protruberant abdomen,
>   vivid red skin with bullae containing many treponemes.

Classification

As stated on p. 29, congenital syphilis can be divided into:
>   early,
>   late,
>   stigmata.

The dividing line between early and late congenital syphilis, like acquired syphilis, is arbitrarily placed at 2 years. This 2-year division is chosen because during the first 2 years the lesions contain many treponemes and are infectious. In the late stage of congenital and acquired syphilis the lesions contain very few treponemes and are not infectious.

The lesions of early congenital syphilis resemble, with certain differences, those of secondary syphilis; the lesions of late congenital syphilis also resemble those of late acquired syphilis, again with differences.

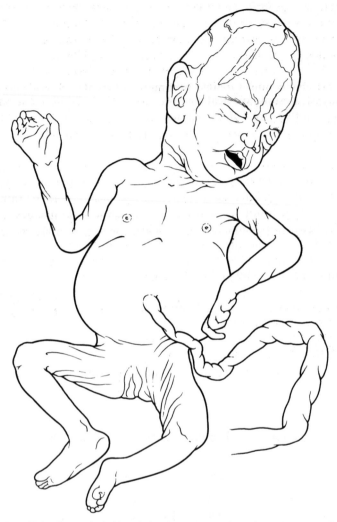

FIG. 7.1   Severely infected dead macerated fetus in early congenital syphilis.

Early congenital syphilis

Clinical features

Rash. Usually the newborn baby appears clinically well. An occasional baby is born with a bullous rash, so-called 'syphilitic impetigo'. The blebs and bullae are mainly on the palms and soles, Only occasionally are other sites affected. The fluid in the bullae may be serous, seropurulent or haemorrhagic and teems with treponemes. (Bullae are not seen in acquired syphilis.)

Failure to thrive and gain weight may be the first clinical feature of early congenital syphilis, becoming apparent 2–8 weeks after birth. Actual weight loss may occur producing a wizened face like that of an old man. When the rash appears after birth it resembles the eruption of secondary syphilis. Details are shown in Figures 7.2 and 7.3.

In moist regions such as the napkin area, the angles of the mouth and around the nostrils, the surface of the papule can become eroded and moist, so-called 'moist papules'. Those around the anus may develop into condylomata lata. Fissures may also develop around the mucocutaneous junctions at the angles of the mouth,

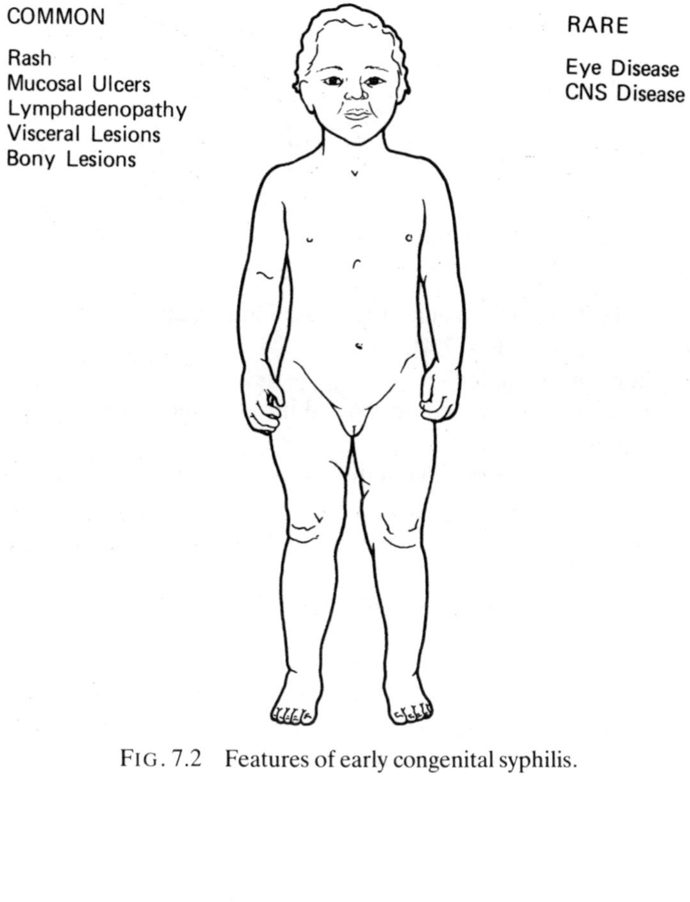

COMMON

Rash
Mucosal Ulcers
Lymphadenopathy
Visceral Lesions
Bony Lesions

RARE

Eye Disease
CNS Disease

FIG. 7.2   Features of early congenital syphilis.

Face
Napkin Area
Palms
Soles

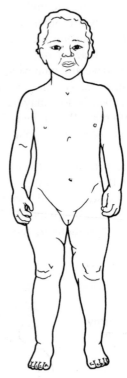

FIG. 7.3   Distribution of rash in early congenital syphilis.

nasolabial folds and around the anus. These heal with linear scars called 'rhagades' (Fig. 7.4).

Other signs include:

brownish-yellow colour of skin: so-called 'cafe au lait' pigmentation,'

patchy hair loss: syphilitic alopecia, (rarely, excess hair: syphilitic wig)

papules at base of nail: syphilitic onychia.

Mucosal ulcers identical with those of secondary syphilis involve;

lips,
mouth,
throat,
larynx,
genital mucous membranes.

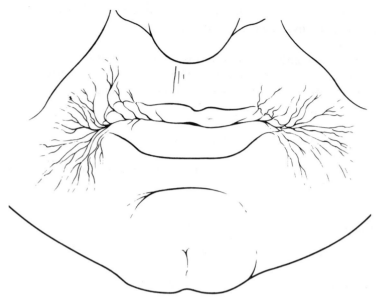

FIG. 7.4   Scars at the angles of mouth (rhagades) are stigmata of congenital syphilis.

Similar lesions affect the nose, but may also involve the underlying periosteum, leading to rhinitis or 'syphilitic snuffles'. Nasal discharge and obstruction occur which may lead to feeding difficulties and weight loss.

Lymphadenopathy may be generalised with rubbery nodes but they remain relatively small.

Visceral lesions notably enlargement of liver and spleen may be so marked that the abdomen is grossly protruberant. Occasionally other viscera may be involved such as the kidneys leading to the nephrotic syndrome.

Bone lesions. Osteochondritis or epiphysitis is characteristic on the first 6 months with periostosis in some cases. The proximal end of the tibia and the distal end of the radius and ulna are the sites commonly involved. So much pain is present that the affected limb is held immobile: 'syphilitic pseudoparalysis'. It is obviously tender to touch and the affected end is swollen. Radiographs show enlargement of the epiphysis, irregular thickening of the distal end of the metaphysis giving it a saw-toothed appearance (Fig. 7.5) and periostosis.

After 6 months osteochondritis disappears but osteoperiostitis becomes more prominent. The proximal phalanges are characteristically involved, hands more often than feet, so called 'syphilitic dactylitis' (Fig. 7.6).

Eyes. Choroidoretinitis occurs but is difficult to see.

CNS involvement. Asymptomatic neurosyphilis is more common than frank meninigitis.

Diagnosis of early congenital syphilis

Dark-ground examination shows *T. pallidum* in serum from:
 bullae,
 papules, especially moist papules,
 mucosal ulcers.

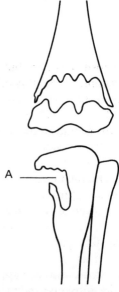

A

FIG. 7.5 Osteochondritis in early congenital syphilis. Lower end of femur shows widened epiphysis with irregular saw-tooth appearance; (A) upper end of tibia shows a lytic area on medial side (Wimberger's sign).

Syphilitic Dactylitis Osteoperiostosis

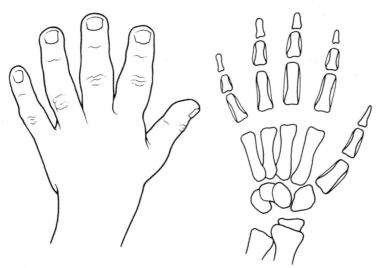

FIG. 7.6   Syphilitic dactylitis due to periostosis of phalanges in early congenital syphilis.

Serological tests may be positive at birth but may take some months to become positive. In a clinically healthy baby in whom congenital syphilis is suspected, repeat the tests at 3, 6, 9 and 12 weeks and at 6 months. A rising VDRL titre with a positive TPHA result is diagnostic. Take blood from all suspected cases but serological tests are not a substitute for dark-ground examinations which must be attempted in all cases with suspicious clinical signs.

Serum antibodies produced by the baby must be distinguished from maternal IgG antibody which can passively cross the placenta. This maternal antibody is present at birth and gradually disappears over about 6–12 weeks. In a clinically healthy baby with serum antibodies present at birth, repeat the tests at 3–6 week intervals until they disappear.

If serum antibodies are present at birth and early diagnosis is important, congenital syphilis may be associated with a higher VDRL titre in baby than in mother. Specific IgM antibody in the neonate may indicate congenital syphilis, but false–positive results occur.

Antitreponemal antimicrobials must not be given while serial tests are being taken.

Radiographs must be taken of all suspect long bones.

CSF must be examined in all cases with neurological features.

Treatment

procaine penicillin 0·5 megaunits i.m. per kg in divided doses
over 10 days,
continue for 15–21 days if there is CNS involvement.
If penicillin hypersensitivity develops or is suspected give:
erythromycin 30–50 mg per kg in divided doses by mouth for 15
days.

Prognosis

Cure rates are at least 90% after one course.

Follow-up

This is similar to other forms of syphilis and is shown in Figure 7.7.
At each visit:
examine clinically,
repeat serological tests.

Differential diagnosis

Failure to thrive may have to be distinguished from the long list of other causes of the problem.

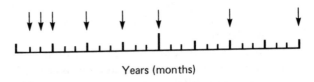

Attendance

Years (months)

In late disease see once a year, after two years

FIG. 7.7   Follow-up after treatment of congenital syphilis.

Bullae must be distinguished from:
    impetigo,
    pemphigus.

Maculopapular lesions may resemble:
    drug rashes,
    scabies,
    eczema,
    tinea,
    insect bites,
    napkin rash.

Snuffles obviously resemble coryza, but blood in the discharge should arouse suspicion.

Mucosal ulceration of the mouth may resemble:
    herpes simplex,
    aphthous ulceration.

Osteochondritis may be mistaken for a fracture.

Syphilitic osteoperiostosis must be distinguished from periostosis and osteomyelitis due to other causes.

Late congenital syphilis

LATE LATENT CONGENITAL SYPHILIS

Latent disease is probably the commonest form of late congenital syphilis. It is diagnosed by serological tests and may be difficult to distinguish from latent acquired syphilis; the family must be examined.

GUMMAS

These usually appear from the age of 5 years. They involve:
    skin,
    subcutaneous tissue,
    palate (more common than in acquired syphilis) (Fig. 7.8),
    nasal septum (more common than in acquired syhilis; characteristic collapse of the nose, Fig. 7.9),
    long bones, osteoperiostosis; sabre tibia (Fig. 7.10).

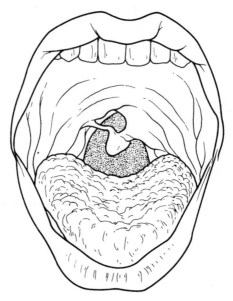

FIG. 7.8   Perforation of the soft palate due to gummatous ulceration in late congenital syphilis.

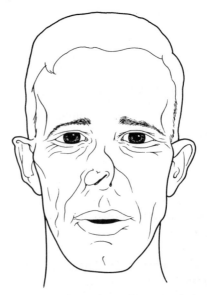

FIG. 7.9   Gummatous destruction of the nasal septum and collapse of lower part of nose in late congenital syphilis.

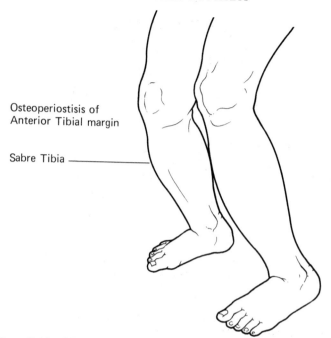

Osteoperiostisis of
Anterior Tibial margin

Sabre Tibia

FIG. 7.10 Clinical appearance of sabre tibia in late congenital syphilis.

NEUROSYPHILIS

This may be asymptomatic. Late congenital neurosyphilis produces the same effects as acquired disease:
        meningeal,
        vascular,
        parenchymatous.

CARDIOVASCULAR DISEASE

This is rare in late congenital syphilis.
    Characteristic, rare and ill-understood features include:
        interstitial keratitis,
        Clutton's joints,
        Hutchinson's triad (Fig. 7.11) of:
                deafness,
                interstitial keratitis,
                Hutchinson's teeth (Fig. 7.12).

They appear to be due to hypersensitivity, for antitreponemal treatment alone fails to produce cure.

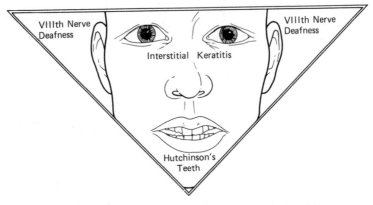

FIG. 7.11 Hutchinson's triad in late congenital syphilis.

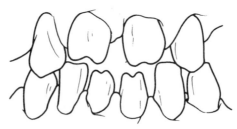

FIG. 7.12 Hutchinson's incisors in late congenital syphilis.

INTERSTITIAL KERATITIS

This is the most common late clinical lesion. It is usually bilateral but starts in one eye before the other. Females may be affected more than males. It may start at any age from 4 years.

At first there is circumcorneal vascularisation of the sclera followed by vascular infiltration and cellular exudation into the deeper layers of the cornea.

Symptoms

> Dimness of vision,
> supraorbital pain,
> photophobia,
> lachrymation.

Signs

> Vasodilatation around cornea,
> cornea develops hazy ground-glass appearance,
> later, cornea may become pink,
> choroidoretinitis is also usually present but is masked by the
> corneal changes.

Early changes can only be seen with a slit lamp; refer all cases to an eye specialist.

Diagnose from the above features, plus positive serological results.

Treatment

> Procaine penicillin 900,000 units daily i.m. for 15 days for
> adults, smaller daily dose according to size and age for
> younger patients,
> prednisone eye drops 2 hourly till symptoms and signs stop (4–5
> days),
> then prednisone eye drops 4 hourly for 4–5 days,
> then prednisone eye drops 4 hourly by day, with
> hydrocortisone eye ointment at night for 4 weeks.

Follow this with hydrocortisone eye ointment twice a day for a further 4 weeks.

Re-start steroids if there is any suggestion of relapse.

Prognosis

Without local corticosteroids relapse is common.

Corneal scarring can occur as grey opacities. In severe cases these may be large, dense and cause blindness.

Residual choroidoretinitis may also cause visual failure.

Slit lamp examination can show 'ghost vessels' of previous interstitial keratitis in apparently normal eyes.

Differential diagnosis

Interstitial keratitis is characteristic and is very rarely due to any other cause.

CLUTTON'S JOINTS

This is painless hydrarthrosis of both knees; it appears from the age of 10 years. No radiological bone changes are seen. Give corticosteroids in addition to antimicrobials.

EIGHTH-NERVE DEAFNESS

This occurs in:
>   late congenital syphilis,
>   early acquired syphilis,
>   late acquired syphilis,

though it is traditionally described under late congenital syphilis. The pathogenesis is not clear. Deafness may occur alone or there may first be tinnitus and deafness resembling Menière's disease. There is progressive high-tone hearing loss, then conversational loss.

Serological tests are positive and the CSF may be normal or abnormal.

Treatment

>   Procaine penicillin 0·9–1·2 megaunits daily i.m. for 15–28 days,
>   or in penicillin hypersensitivity:
>   erythromycin 2–3 g daily in divided oral doses for 21–28 days,
>   prednisone 10 mg three times a day for 4 weeks.

If improvement occurs, it starts within a month; prednisone should be very gradually reduced over 3–6 months. Sometimes a small daily dose of prednisone is required long term. If so, give a course of antimicrobial once a year. If relapse threatens, increase the dose of prednisone and give a further course of antimicrobial.

If no improvement occurs after a month of prednisone reduce by 5 mg daily and stop.

It is not clear what proportion of cases respond to this regime.

Differential diagnosis

Distinguish:
- cutaneous and subcutaneous gummas from:
  - chronic skin infections,
  - tumours,
  - varicose ulcers,
- neurosyphilis from the lesions mentioned under acquired neurosyphilis,
- interstitial keratitis is rarely due to any other cause,
- Clutton's joints from other causes of chronic arthritis and synovitis such as:
  - rheumatoid arthritis,
  - psoriatic arthritis,
  - Reiter's disease (Chapter 11),
  - tuberculous arthritis,
- eighth nerve deafness from:
  - accoustic trauma,
  - Meniere's disease,
- osteoperiostosis from:
  - osteomyelitis,
  - Paget's disease.

Stigmata of congenital syphilis

The stigmata or characteristic scars of congenital syphilis are shown in Tables 7.1 and 7.2.

TABLE 7.1 Stigmata of early lesions in congenital syphilis.

Saddle nose	Rhinitis impairs growth and development of nasal bones (Fig. 7.13).
Bulldog face	Rhinitis impairs development of maxillae producing a high palate and depressed bridge of the nose, and relative prominence of lower jaw (Fig. 7.13).
Rhagades	Most lesions leading to linear and other scars at angles of mouth and nostrils (Fig. 7.4).
Hutchinson's teeth	Failure of development of central tooth bud (Fig. 7.12).
Moon's or mulberry molars	Failure of development of first lower molar (Fig. 7.14).

TABLE 7.2 Stigmata of late lesions of congenital syphilis.

Corneal opacities	and ghost vessels following interstitial keratitis.
Choroidoretinitis	which may cause visual failure
Gummatous scars	on skin resembling tertiary syphilis,
	scarring and deformity of pharynx,
	perforations of nasal septum (sometimes characteristic nasal collapse, Fig. 7.9),
Sabre tibia	and other healed gummatous osteoperiostoses of long bones (Fig. 7.10)
Frontal and parital bossing of skull due to healed bony disease.	
Optic atrophy	
Nerve deafness	

Diagnosis of late congenital syphilis

In general, diagnosis can be made from:
> the clinical picture,
> results of serological tests which follow the same pattern as in acquired syphilis,
> CSF results,
> special investigations, such as biopsy of gummas.

Antimicrobial treatment for late congenital syphilis

This also follows the general pattern as for acquired syphilis, namely:
> procaine penicillin 600,000 units i.m. daily for 15 days for adults, 900,000 units i.m. daily for larger individuals,
> smaller doses for young patients according to age and size: continue for 21 days if there is CNS involvement.

In penicillin hypersensitivity give:
> oxytetracycline or erythromycin, 2–3 g daily in divided doses for 15 days, continue for 21–28 days if there is CNS disease.

Follow-up

Initially this is the same as for early congenital syphilis, but the patient should be seen annually after 2 years.

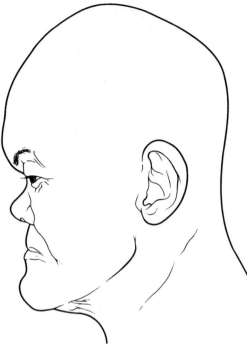

FIG. 7.13 Bulldog face with saddle nose and relative prominence of lower jaw in late congenital syphilis.

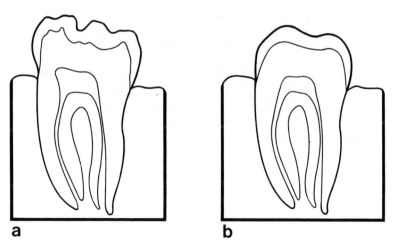

a   **b**

FIG. 7.14 Moon's molars in late congenital syphilis: (a) normal, (b) abnormal.

CHAPTER 8

Gonorrhoea

Cause

Gonorrhoea is caused by the Gram-negative diplococcus *Neisseria gonorrhoeae* or gonococcus (Fig. 8.1).

The organism invades columnar epithelium, classically in the anterior urethra in heterosexual males. Other sites invaded are shown in Table 8.1.

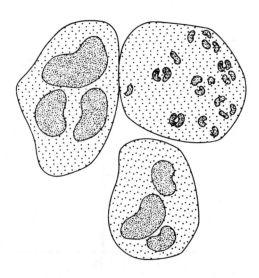

FIG. 8.1 Intracellular diplococci shown in upper left leucocyte in gonorrhoea.

TABLE 8.1   Sites the gonococcus invades.

Site	Condition	Type of patient
Anterior urethra	Gonococcal urethritis, Urethral gonorrhoea,	Heterosexual men, Homosexual men.
Rectum	Gonococcal proctitis, Rectal gonorrhoea,	Homosexual men, Women.
Endocervical canal Urethra	Endocervicitis, Urethritis,	Women
Pharynx	Gonococcal pharyngitis, Pharyngeal gonorrhoea,	Mainly homosexual men, less often women, rarely heterosexual men.
Conjunctiva	Ophthalmia neonatorum, Gonococcal conjunctivitis,	Newborn babies, Adults (rare).
Vulva and vagina	Gonococcal vulvo-vaginitis,	Only in pre-pubertal girls

In men invasion of the anterior urethral mucosa usually leads to symptoms, and in the newborn conjunctival invasion usually produces symptoms; invasion of other sites is often without symptoms until complications develop.

Incubation period

In men with gonococcal urethritis this is usually 2–5 days with extremes of 1–10 days.

In the newborn with conjunctival infection, it is usually 2–5 days, but may be 13 days.

Presentation of gonococcal urethritis in men

Sudden onset,
burning, scalding discomfort on micturition,
purulent urethral discharge (Fig. 8.2).

OTHER CLINICAL FEATURES. On examination, in addition to the discharge, there is:

injection of the meatal mucosa.

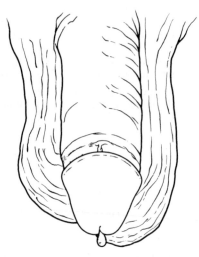

FIG. 8.2   Gonococcal urethritis.

Occasionally there is also:
    erythema of the glans penis,
    enlarged inguinal nodes.
The lymph nodes are slightly to moderately enlarged and may be tender.

    In symptom-free men, who form up to 5 per cent of all men with urethral gonorrhoea, a discharge may be found on careful examination.

Clinical features of genital gonorrhoea in women

As already stated, there may be no symptoms (in about 50 per cent to a maximum of 75 per cent of women with uncomplicated gonorrhoea). When they occur, symptoms are commonly:
    dysuria,
    vaginal discharge.
These are common symptoms in women and may not disturb a woman enough to see a doctor. Furthermore, a non-specialist doctor may not consider gonorrhoea as a possible cause of these symptoms. In contrast, the symptoms of gonococcal urethritis in a man usually alerts him and his doctor to the possibility of urethritis.

On examination, a female with genital gonorrhoea may show:
no abnormality,
mucoid or purulent discharge from the cervical os,
rarely, a frank urethral discharge.

Vaginal discharge alone is more likely to be due to concomitant trichomoniasis; this occurs commonly with gonorrhoea in women, especially Negro women, and may be the cause of the symptoms.

Clinical features of rectal gonorrhoea

This is often without symptoms. When present they may be:
rectal discharge,
tenesmus.
On examination via a proctoscope there is:
often no abnormality,
rarely, there is florid proctitis with:
purulent discharge,
injected mucosa.

Clinical features of pharyngeal gonorrhoea

This also rarely produces symptoms, but occasionally the patient may complain of a sore throat. On examination, appearances are usually normal; occasionally there is marked pharyngitis or tonsillitis.

Clinical features of gonococcal conjunctivitis/ophthalmia neonatorum in the newborn

In the newborn, this usually produces brisk conjunctivitis with:
purulent discharge,
conjunctival inflammation,
occasional orbital oedema.
Exceptionally, the same symptoms occur in adults who are infected by carrying organisms from the genitals on the hands.

Clinical features of vulvovaginitis

Pre-pubertal girls have immature vulval and vaginal epithelium which is susceptible to invasion by the gonococcus. This usually only occurs when there is overcrowding and faulty personal hygiene.

There may be:
    no symptoms,
    vaginal discharge,
    redness and swelling of the vulva.

Investigations and diagnosis

The clinical features of gonorrhoea are not clear cut and a clinical diagnosis *cannot* be made. Diagnosis depends on results of laboratory investigations as outlined in Chapter 3. These are:
    recognising typical Gram-negative diplococci in stained smears of secretion (as shown in Fig. 8.1).
    This leads to rapid presumptive diagnosis in the clinic.
    Identifying *N. gonorrhoeae* in cultures. This provides confirmation in the laboratory.
The collection of samples for investigation is summarised in Table 8.2.

In urethral gonorrhoea, in men, Gram-stained smears of infected secretion are accurate in at least 95 per cent of cases, but cultures should still be taken for:
    full identification,
    antimicrobial sensitivity tests.
It is normal to rely on results of one smear and culture, and initial treatment is based on the results of the Gram-stained smear.
    The two-glass urine test shows:
    first glass   :   haze and specks,
    second glass   :   clear.
In severe cases, a slight haze and a few specks may be seen in the second glass indicating that not all the inflammatory exudate has been washed out into the first glass; these changes should rapidly clear with treatment.

In women, Gram-stained smears are more difficult to interpret as many other organisms are present and they may be positive in only about 60 per cent of cases. It is necessary to wait for the results of cultures before starting treatment in the remaining cases. When gonorrhoea is strongly suspected as in female contacts of infected men, repeat smears and cultures from the urethral meatus, cervical os and rectum once or twice to diagnose or exclude gonorrhoea.

The same principles apply to vulvovaginitis in girls and rectal infection in men.

The pharynx harbours saprophytic neisseria and meningococci. Gram-stained smears cannot be relied upon, and the diagnosis must await results of laboratory cultures including full and careful identification of neisseria species.

In untreated purulent conjunctivitis the Gram-stained smears usually show typical organisms. Cultures, however, must be taken for confirmation.

As indicated in Chapter 3, special selective antibiotic-containing media should be used to culture gonococci wherever possible, especially in samples from rectum, throat and female genitalia.

TABLE 8.2 Sites sampled

Men	Urethral meatus, Rectum, Pharynx.
Women	Urethral meatus, Cervical os, Rectum, Pharynx.
Babies (and adults with conjunctivitis)	Conjunctival secretion.

Note: Smears for Gram staining, and cultures, are taken from *all* sites except the pharynx, where cultures alone are taken.

Complications

These may be:
> local or general,
> acute or chronic.

LOCAL COMPLICATIONS. These may involve any structure lined by columnar epithelium and communicating with an original site of infection.

ACUTE LOCAL COMPLICATIONS IN MEN. These are listed
in Table 8.3.

TABLE 8.3   Acute local complications of
anterior urethritis in men.

Infection of paraurethral ducts,
Tysonitis,
Infection of ducts and glands of Littre,
Posterior urethritis,
Prostatitis,
Vasitis,
Vesiculitis,
Epididymitis (Fig. 8.3),
Orchitis.
Rarely, infection of:
Median raphe of penis,
Periurethral tissues leading to abscess
formation,
Cowper's ducts and glands.

Epididymitis (Fig. 8.3). This is the most important of the
complications listed in Table 8.3. The condition is usually unilateral
and associated with vasitis.

The patient presents complaining of:
pain,
and usually: urethral discharge,
dysuria.
On examination there is:
markedly tender swelling of the epididymis,
tender swelling of the vas deferens,
variable amount of effusion into the tunica vaginalis,
a normal testis.
Sometimes the effusion is so tense the testis and epididymis cannot
be palpated. In the occasional severe case, the testis is also infected,
becoming swollen and tender; this condition is epididymoorchitis.

Littritis. This occurs in all cases of anterior urethritis and is
important only in the occasional case in which there is rupture
leading to spread into periurethral tissues. This in turn may
produce:
abscess,
later stricture.

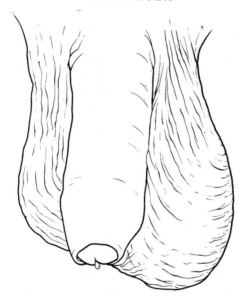

FIG. 8.3 Acute left epididymitis.

Such problems only arise in neglected cases or if instruments (endoscope or bougie) are passed during active urethritis.

A periurethral abscess presents as a painful swelling in the shaft of the penis.

Posterior urethritis. This probably occurs to some degree in many cases of anterior urethritis, especially if treatment is delayed. It is present in:

> most cases of epididymitis,
> all cases of prostatitis.

Posterior urethritis is associated with more marked urinary symptoms.

Acute prostatitis. Clinical acute prostatitis has become rare since the discovery of antimicrobials and usually only occurs if treatment is delayed. Patients present with:

> marked urinary symptoms,
> malaise,
> perineal discomfort.

On examination, there may be:
    fever,
    urethral discharge.
And on rectal examination, the prostate is:
    swollen,
    tense,
    acutely tender.
Occasionally, an abscess may form with a general increase in all these features, plus:
    tenesmus,
    constipation.
Rectal gonorrhoea may be complicated by abscesses around the rectum. Other acute complications of gonorrhoea in men are extremely rare.

CHRONIC LOCAL COMPLICATIONS IN MEN. These do not occur if prompt, effective antimicrobial therapy is obtained.

Urethral stricture. This is the most important chronic local complication. The patient complains of:
    obstructive symptoms, namely:
        difficulty in starting micturition,
        poor stream,
        dribbling at the end of micturition,
    frequency,
    urgency,
    perhaps pain.
In addition there may be:
    recurrent urinary infection with dysuria,
    recurrent urethritis with:
        dysuria,
        discharge.
Investigations needed include:
    microscopy and culture of discharge for micro-organisms and
        trichomonads,
    urine culture,
    intravenous urogram,
    urethrogram,
    endoscopy.

Chronic prostatitis. This is considered with prostatovesiculitis under non-gonococcal infection (p. 135).

ACUTE LOCAL COMPLICATIONS IN WOMEN. The common acute local complications are shown in Table 8.4.

TABLE 8.4 Acute local complications of genital gonorrhoea in women.

Skenitis,
Bartholinitis (Fig. 8.4),
Salpingitis, and pelvic infection or
    pelvic inflammatory disease (PID)
    (they usually co-exist) (Fig. 8.5),
Rarely, cystitis.

Skenitis. This produces pain and swelling underlying the opening of the ducts which are beside the meatus or nearby. Skenitis usually resolves with the treatment of uncomplicated infection; if neglected, an abscess or cyst may form.

Bartholinitis (Fig. 8.4). Bartholin's glands are situated in the lower half of the labia majora and the ducts open on the medial side of the labia minora. If an infected duct becomes blocked an abscess forms.
The patient complains of:
    pain,
    genital swelling,
    difficulty in walking.
On examination there is:
    swelling,
    fluctuation may be present,
    pus may be seen at the opening of the duct.
The diagnosis is made from clinical features and the results of Gram stain and culture of pus expressed from the duct or aspirated from an abscess. If these are negative then the diagnosis rests on the results of the routine Gram stains and culture from urethra, cervix and rectum which must be taken in all cases. Initially, treatment should be based on the Gram-stain results.

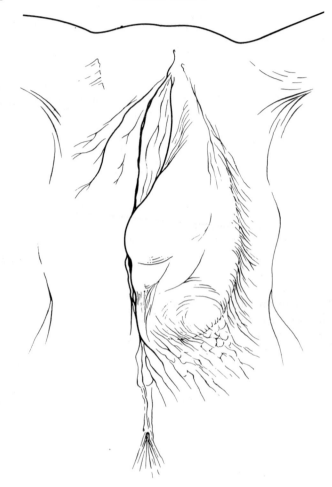

FIG. 8.4   Acute left bartholinitis.

Salpingitis and pelvic infection. These are regarded here as one
condition (Fig. 8.5). It still appears to occur in about 15 per cent of
women who acquire gonorrhoea in developed countries and 10 per
cent of these women are left with impaired fertility. Pelvic infection
and resulting subfertility is much more common in certain countries
of the Third World. Prompt recogntion and energetic management
is vital. The condition is more common in women fitted with an
intrauterine contraceptive device (IUCD) and less common in
women taking oral contraceptives.

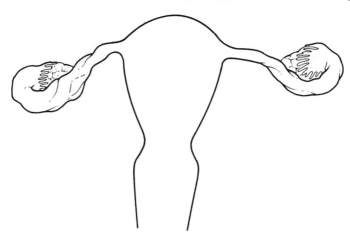

FIG. 8.5   Acute bilateral salpingitis.

The onset is commonly just after or during a menstrual period. The patient complains of pain, often cramping, and menstrual irregularity (if not taking oral contraceptives).

Other symptoms are:
   malaise,
   nausea,
   vomiting.

Abdominal examination shows:
   lower abdominal tenderness,
   rarely, guarding,
      rebound tenderness.

Vaginal examination:
   tenderness usually in one or both lateral fornices,
   cervical excitation produces pain,
   sometimes fullness in a lateral or the posterior fornix,
   sometimes a mass.

There is often a low-grade fever.

The diagnosis depends on the clinical features and finding presumptive gonococci in Gram stains of secretion taken from urethra, cervix and rectum. Again, the start of treatment is based on Gram-stain results and it should not be delayed while culture results are awaited, though cultures must be taken.

If there is doubt about the clinical features, refer the patient to a gynaecologist for laparoscopy.

CHRONIC LOCAL COMPLICATIONS IN WOMEN. As in men, chronic complications are rare in Britain and usually only occur when treatment of acute complications is inadequate.

Chronic skenitis and bartholinitis. These can be readily recognised from the history and the swelling.

Chronic pelvic infection. This causes much misery, invalidism and infertility. There is:
    menstrual irregularity,
    dysmenorrhoea,
    dyspareunia,
    lower abdominal pain,
    low-grade fever,
    malaise,
    recurrent attacks of pelvic infection.
On examination there is:
    lower abdominal tenderness,
    pelvic tenderness.
There may be:
    deviation of cervix due to adhesions,
    pelvic mass due to hydrosalpinx,
    pyosalpnx,
    tubo-ovarian abscess.
Laparoscopy should be undertaken, where possible, to confirm the diagnosis.

GENERAL COMPLICATIONS OF GONORRHOEA. These are rare and are more common in women. They comprise:
    bacteraemia,
    septicaemia,
    perihepatitis,
    arthritis.

Gonococcal bacteraemia (benign gonococcaemia). This is often due to gonococci with a particular biotype. The gonococci have particular growth requirements including a need for arginine, hypoxanthine and uracil; sometimes this is called the AHU auxotype. They are also usually very sensitive to penicillin. The prevalence of bacteraemia varies with the prevalence of the biotype of gonococci. The patients who develop this complication may have a minor immunological deficiency.

Pregnancy, especially in its second half, appears to be a predisposing factor. In the non-pregnant woman the illness starts during or just after menstruation.

The characteristic features are:
    fever,
    joint pains,
    rash.
The fever tends to be low grade and intermittent. Initially, the joint pains tend to be widespread but asymmetrical. Later, sub-acute arthritis settles in one to three of the following:
    wrists,
    knees,
    ankles,
    elbows,
    small joints of the hand.
Tenosynovitis may be present.

The rash tends to occur in crops which coincide with the fever. There are few lesions (15 to 20) which tend to occur peripherally on the limbs, often over joints but not necessarily the affected joints. They pass rapidly through the following stages:
    macule,
    papule,
    vesicopustule,
    haemorrhagic pustule.
They heal after 3–4 days leaving brownish discolouration.

Diagnosis is based on the clinical picture and identification of *N. gonorrhoeae*. The organism is readily identified in secretion from:
    urethra,
    cervix,
    rectum.
Sometimes the initial site of infection is the pharynx, and a throat swab must be taken in all cases. It is very difficult to culture gonococci from blood, synovial fluid or pus from pustules, though this should be attempted in all cases; specific immunofluorescent staining has given positive results in this material confirming the cause of the condition. Remember, gonococci causing bacteraemia may be very sensitive to penicillin, so ask the bacteriologist to use non-antibiotic medium as well as selective medium.

Gonococcal septicaemia. This is a serious condition causing;
> endocarditis,
> myocarditis,
> pericarditis,
> meningitis.

Its recognition depends on isolating gonococci from blood cultures.

Gonococcal perihepatitis (Fitz–Hugh Curtis syndrome). This is more common in females with a history of pelvic infection. Spread is said to be:
> directly upwards along the paracolic gutters,
> via the retroperitoneal lymphatics,
> via the blood stream (the most likely route).

The patients complain of:
> pain in the right upper abdomen, which is worse on deep breathing, coughing or flexing of the trunk,
> sometimes pain in the right shoulder,
> nausea,
> vomiting.

On examination, there is:
> tenderness in the right upper abdomen,
> fever.

Diagnosis is based on:
> clinical findings,
> identifying gonococci in genital secretions,
> chest radiograph, which may show right pleural effusion,
> routine investigations, such as serum liver function tests, which are usually normal.

Rarely, gonococci may be cultured from the blood.

Laparoscopy (if available) shows adhesions between the liver and the anterior abdominal wall and diaphragm.

Gonococcal arthritis. This is an acute septic arthritis in which gonococci are identified in the synovial fluid.

Differential diagnosis

In adults with uncomplicated gonorrhoea, differentiate the following:
> urethral gonorrhoea in men from non-specific urethritis (Chapter 10).

Genital gonorrhoea in women from:
    trichomoniasis (Chapter 12),
    candidosis (Chapter 13),
    urinary infection,
    non-specific genital infection (Chapter 10).
Rectal gonorrhoea from:
    proctitis due to other causes,
    ischiorectal and related abscesses,
Pharyngeal gonorrhoea from:
    tonsillitis,
    pharyngitis.

Gonorrhoea must be distinguished from some of the most common conditions affecting these sites.

, In adults and children, distinguish gonococcal from other causes of conjunctivitis.

In girls, distinguish gonococcal from other causes of vulvovaginitis, such as thread worms.

In general, distinction depends on results of:
    Gram stains,
    cultures.

The differential diagnosis of the complications is shown in Tables 8.5 and 8.6.

TABLE 8.5 Differential diagnosis of local complications.

Epididymitis	Non-gonococcal epididymitis (younger men), Coliform epididymitis (older men).
Prostatitis	Non-gonococcal prostatitis, Tuberculous prostatitis, Urethral stricture, Carcinoma of prostate and bladder.
Pelvic infection	Non-gonococcal pelvic infection, Urinary infection, Appendicitis, Tubal pregnancy, Pain from IUCD, Constipation.

TABLE   8.6 Differential   diagnosis   of   general
                    complications.

Bacteraemia	Meningococcal bacteraemia, *Moraxella* bacteraemia, Low-grade staphylococcal septicaemia
Septicaemia	Other pyogenic septicaemias.
Perihepatitis	Hepatitis due to other causes, Cholecystitis, Peptic ulceration.
Arthritis	Acute arthritis due to other organisms.

CHAPTER 9

Management of gonorrhoea

The management of gonorrhoea, like all other STDs must follow the principles shown in Table 9.1.

TABLE 9.1   Principles of management.

Accurate diagnosis,
Effective treatment,
Careful follow-up,
Rapid contact tracing,
Sexual abstinence.

Accurate diagnosis has been considered in the previous chapter. In men with urethral gonorrhoea the incubation period is shorter so the contacts who are at risk are usually those in the preceeding 2 weeks. Often the infecting contact can be readily identified.

Patients should be urged to abstain from intercourse for 2 weeks after treatment. Some may find this extremely difficult, but it is vital to ensure patients are not infectious before they resume intercourse. The remainder of this chapter is concerned with antimicrobial treatment and follow-up.

Antimicrobial treatment

Gonorrhoea is one of the few infections that responds to a single dose of antimicrobial, provided it is:

an adequate dose,
a suitable drug.

Penicillin

Penicillin is still the drug of first choice because:
>   it is highly effective in most cases,
>   a single dose is effective,
>   it is cheap,
>   it is safe.

When penicillin was first discovered, a small dose was effective but over the years many isolates of gonococci have become less sensitive. It is now generally considered that isolates requiring a minimum inhibitory concentration of 0.125 μg/ml or more are *partially resistant*, or have *reduced sensitivity* to penicillin. Such strains tend to be more common in certain parts of the world, such as Africa and the Far East, where antimicrobials are freely available and organisms tend to be exposed to low concentrations of these drugs (Fig. 9.1). The proportion of such strains also varies with time. At the moment in Britain 20–25 per cent of isolates are partially resistant. Such strains respond to penicillin provided a large enough dose is given. Partial resistance to other antibiotics is associated with partial resistance to penicillin. The property of partial resistance is chromosomally mediated.

In 1976, strains of gonococci were first isolated capable of producing penicillinase and so totally resistant to penicillin. This

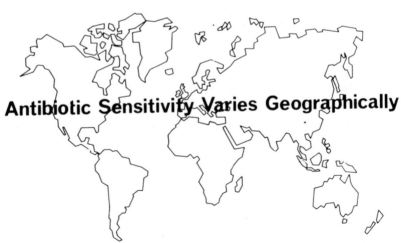

FIG. 9.1 Antimicrobial sensitivity of *N. gonorrhoeae* varies geographically.

property was due to extrachromosomal DNA, so-called R factor. Such strains first appeared in Africa and the Far East, but became established in Europe in 1979. This is potentially a much more serious problem. Though these strains are increasing in numbers, penicillin is still the drug of first choice in the treatment of gonorrhoea.

Exceptions to the use of penicillin are:

patients with known or suspected hypersensitivity to penicillin,
patients in whom treponemal disease is suspected.

Probenecid, which blocks the renal secretion of penicillin, is usually given to provide higher concentrations. It also has the advantages of being cheap and safe.

The treatment recommended for uncomplicated genital and rectal gonorrhoea is shown in Tables 9.2 and 9.3.

Pharyngeal gonorrhoea

This may be more difficult to eradicate than genital and rectal gonorrhoea. A suitable regime is:

ampicillin 2–3·5 g plus probenecid 2 g orally, then:
ampicillin 0·5 g 6-hourly for eight doses, or:
co-trimoxazole four tablets twice a day for 4 days.

TABLE 9.2 Recommended regimens of penicillin for uncomplicated genital and rectal gonorrhoea.

A	Aqueous procaine penicillin 2·4 megaunits i.m. with probenecid 1–2 g orally.
B	Ampicillin 2 g orally with probenecid 1–2 g orally.
C	Ampicillin 3·5 g orally with probenecid 1–2 g orally.
D	Benzyl penicillin 5 megaunits i.m. with probenecid 1–2 g orally.
E	Aqueous procaine penicillin 4·8 megaunits i.m. with probenecid 1–2 g orally.

Treatments A and B give satisfactory results in the UK and other places with comparatively small proportions of partially penicillin resistant gonococci.

Treatments C, D and E give satisfactory results where there are higher proportions of gonococci with partial penicillin resistance.

In treatment D it is usual to give the probenecid 15–30 min before the penicillin. Make up the penicillin in 8 ml 0·5% lignocaine.

TABLE 9.3 Recommended non-penicillin regimens for uncomplicated genital and rectal gonorrhoea.

A	Co-trimoxazole, eight dispersible tablets as a single oral dose.
B	Kanamycin 2 g i.m.
C	Spectinomycin 2–4 g i.m.

All three regimens can be given to patients who are hypersensitive to penicillin.

Treatments A and B are non-treponemacidal, but treatment C may mask treponemal disease and should be avoided when this is suspected.

Take care with kanamycin, see under toxic effects of these regimes.

Gonococcal conjunctivitis/ophthalmia neonatorum of the newborn

Give crystalline penicillin 200,000 units i.m. 6 hourly for 3 days, chloramphenicol eye ointment 6 hourly for 3 days or longer if response is slow.

Conjunctivitis in adults

Treat this with one of the regimes shown in Tables 9.2 and 9.3 plus chloramphenicol eye ointment 6 hourly.

Toxic and side effects with these regimens

Aqueous procaine penicillin, especially in large doses, such as 4·8 megaunits, may inadvertently be injected into the circulation producing alarming hypertensive, manic, procaine reactions quite different from hypersensitivity reactions to penicillin which may also occur.

Probenecid produces heartburn in a few patients.

Ampicillin in 2–3·5 g doses may be associated with a few loose stools. Hypersensitivity rashes may occur.

Co-trimoxazole in single doses appears remarkably free from reactions but occasionally the usual sulphonamide reactions appear.

Kanamycin must be used with care because of the dangers of damage to the VIIIth cranial nerve and the kidney. It should be avoided in patients with any suggestion of such pre-existing disease.

Spectinomycin appears to be remarkably free of unwanted effects, apart from occasional slight discomfort at the injection site.

Follow-up after treatment

The timing of visits is shown in Table 9.4.

TABLE 9.4   Attendance after treatment of uncomplicated gonorrhoea.

1–3 Days after treatment,
7 Days after treatment,
14 Days after treatment.

Examine the patients clinically at each visit. In addition, undertake the investigations outlined.

Men with urethral gonorrhoea

These men should hold their urine for at least 3 hours before attending, preferably overnight. At each visit investigate the patient as follows:

at first visit:	always take a urethral swab for Gram stain and culture.
at subsequent visits:	ideally take a urethral swab at every visit; in practice it is usually sufficient to take a swab if there is a visible urethral discharge.
at every visit:	examine the urine by the two-glass test, see below.

Two-glass urine test. Urine in the first glass usually shows haze with specks before treatment. The haze should rapidly clear; usually at the first visit after treatment. The specks are replaced by threads which in turn disappear. The second glass should be clear throughout follow-up.

Women

At each visit:
> examine clinically,
> collect secretion for Gram stain and culture from:
>> urethra,
>> cervix,
>> rectum, if positive for gonococci before treatment.

It is good practice to repeat investigations for trichomonads and candida at least once after treatment.

Treatment failure

It is always difficult and sometimes impossible to distinguish treatment failure from re-infection. One simple rule is to regard treatment failure as the reappearance of gonococci during the 14 days after treatment in a patient who denies any further sexual contact. Reappearance of gonococci in any other circumstances is regarded as due to re-infection.

Some specialists make no attempt to make a distinction; this means treating all cases as treatment failures.

If re-infection can be established, then the initial treatment can be repeated and the patient firmly advised against futher intercourse.

Treatment failure is usually diagnosed before results of antimicrobial sensitivity tests are available. It is therefore wise to choose treatments which are adequate for partial or total penicillin resistance, such as:
> spectinomycin 2–4 g i.m.,
> cefoxitin 2 g i.m. plus probenecid 1 g by mouth,
> cefuroxime 1·5 g i.m. plus probenecid 1 g.

Both spectinomycin and the cephalosporins are expensive drugs, so should not be used unnecessarily.

Treatment of local complications in men

Acute epididymitis

Give the standard initial dose, such as:
> ampicillin 2 g plus probenecid 1 g,

then:

> ampicillin 500 mg 6-hourly for 7–10 days (plus probenecid 0·5 g 6-hourly if partial penicillin resistance is suspected).

The patient is more comfortable with a scrotal support and mild analgesics may be indicated. It is traditional to advise against heavy lifting which may cause reflux of urine into the vas deferens, but the need for this advice is debatable. In the patient hypersensitive to penicillin, give:

> co-trimoxazole 8 (dispersible) tablets initially,

then:

> co-trimoxazole two tablets twice a day for 7–10 days.

Prostatitis

Acute prostatitis. Give antimicrobial therapy as for acute epididymitis but continue for 14–21 days. Acute urinary retention may be relieved by a hot bath and micturition while in the bath. Catheterisation should be avoided if possible.

Chronic prostatitis is usually non-gonococcal and is considered under non-specific genital infection, see page 135.

Urethral stricture

Refer the patient to a urologist for dilatation or urethroplasty.

Local complications in women

Skenitis

Skenitis usually responds to routine therapy as for uncomplicated infection. Destroy the chronically infected Skene's gland with electrocautery.

Acute bartholinitis

Give the usual single dose of antimicrobial and if there is an abscess aspirate it under local anaesthesia. If it recurs refer the patient to a gynaecologist for marsupialisation, after further chemotherapy.

Acute pelvic infection

This demands prompt and vigorous treatment. The principles are:
  antimicrobials,
  rest.
  Give:
    benzyl penicillin 5 megaunits i.m. plus probenecid 1 g orally,
followed by:
    benzyl penicillin 1 megaunit i.m. (plus probenecid 0·5 g orally
      depending on probability of penicillin partial resistance).
until all symptoms and signs, including pelvic tenderness, have
resolved—usually 2–4 days. Then give:
    procaine penicillin 1·2 megaunits i.m. 12-hourly to complete 10
      days treatment.
As an alternative give:
    ampicillin 2–3·5 g plus probenecid 1–2 g orally,
followed by:
    ampicillin 0·5–1 g±probenecid 0·5 g 6-hourly for 10 days.
For the patient who is hypersensitive to penicillin give:
    co-trimoxazole four tablets twice a day until all symptoms and
      signs have resolved,
followed by:
    co-trimoxazole two tablets twice a day to complete 10 days
      treatment.
  Penicillinase-producing gonococci can produce pelvic infection.
If such an organism is reported by the laboratory, start treatment
with:
    cefuroxime 1·5 g i.m. plus probenecid 1 g orally,
followed by:
    cefuroxime 0·75 g 8-hourly until all symptoms and signs have
      resolved.
Then continue with an oral antimicrobial as indicated by *in-vitro*
sensitivity results to complete 10 days therapy.
  If the condition is severe, the patient should be admitted
to hospital for bed rest and should remain in bed, except for toilet
purposes, until all symptoms and signs have resolved. Less severe
cases may rest in bed at home.
  Occasionally, it may be necessary to drain a pelvic abscess and
this is best done by a gynaecologist.
  Pelvic infection is commoner in women fitted with an IUCD than
in other women. Opinion is divided concerning leaving or removing

what is effectively a foreign body. If response to treatment is satisfactory in a first attack of pelvic infection, the device can be left safely *in situ*.

Some cases of pelvic infection are due to chlamydial, or gonococcal plus chlamydial, infection. If response to the above antimicrobial treatment is unsatisfactory, consider changing to:

oxytetracycline 500 mg four times a day for 14 days.

There is evidence that the addition of corticosteroids assist in ensuring patency of the Fallopian tubes, but whether these function is debatable.

Chronic pelvic infection also needs energetic treatment. This includes:

rest,

antimicrobials, such as ampicillin 500 mg four times a day for 14–28 days,

short-wave diathermy may help.

The condition is liable to recur and ultimately surgical removal may be necessary.

Treatment of generalised complications

Bacteraemia

Treat as for acute pelvic infection, but continue treatment for 14 days. Aspirate any moderate or large effusion.

Septicaemia

Start therapy with intravenous benzyl penicillin 2 megaunits 4-hourly until symptoms and signs have settled. Then continue antimicrobials as for acute pelvic infection but continue for 14 days.

If there is evidence of cardiac involvement, prolonged rest is indicated; obtain advice of a cardiologist.

If there is meningitis, a neurologist should be consulted.

Gonococcal perihepatitis

Treat like gonococcal bacteraemia.

Acute gonococcal arthritis

Treat as follows:

>   antimicrobials as for gonococcal bacteraemia initially,
>   complete rest for the affected joint; a light splint may be indicated,
>   aspirate any moderate or large effusion,
>   once resolution is proceeding satisfactorily, start gentle passive movements, then active movements,
>   give analgesics in the acute phase,
>   consider giving an anti-inflammatory agent, such as indomethacin, if progress is slow.

Prognosis of gonorrhoea

The principles outlined should lead to satisfactory cure rates.

In uncomplicated gonorrhoea 95 per cent of cases should respond to the initial therapy.

The remainder respond to a second dose, very occasionally a third dose is needed.

Acute complications usually respond to initial therapy.

Chronic complications. Response depends on duration and severity.

CHAPTER 10

Non-specific genital infection

Urethral inflammation can be classified as:
    gonococcal,
    non-gonococcal, or non-specific.

The terms non-gonococcal and non-specific are often loosely used synonymously but non-gonococcal means that only gonorrhoea has been excluded, while non-specific strictly implies that all known possible causes have been excluded, though this is not usually the case. The latter name is adopted here as it has become widely used despite the inaccuracy. The term non-specific genital infection covers:
    non-specific or non-gonococcal urethritis in men,
    non-specific or non-gonococcal infection in women.

In addition, this chapter considers non-specific or non-gonococcal proctitis, non-gonococcal ophthalmia and pulmonary infection.

Non-specific urethritis in men

Non-specific urethritis or NSU is the most common condition found in men attending clinics in Britain, and it is now recognised in many other countries to be as prevalent, and perhaps more prevalent, than gonorrhoea.

Aetiology

It is widely accepted that *Chlamydia trachomatis*, the cause of trachoma and inclusion conjunctivitis (hence its earlier name TRIC agent) causes about 50 per cent of cases of NSU. A very small proportion, about 5 per cent, are due to the various possible causes listed in Table 10.1. The cause of the remaining 45 per cent is not clear. *C. trachomatis* may cause more infections for isolation techniques may at present be insensitive.

TABLE 10.1   Causes of NSU.

Probable infective agent	*Chlamydia trachomatis.*
Other possible organisms	*Ureaplasma urealyticum,*
Other possible causes (rare)	*Haemophilus vaginalis (Gardnerella vaginalis).*
	Upper urinary infection,
	Trichomoniasis,
	Candidosis,
	Trauma,
	Foreign bodies,
	Urethral stricture,
	Warts,
	Syphilis,
	Herpes simplex virus,
	Other bacteria,
	Neoplasms,
	Crystalluria,
	Hypersensitivity.

CHLAMYDIA. Chlamydia possess characteristics of bacteria and viruses. They are obligate intracellular parasites and can only be grown in the laboratory in cell cultures (Fig. 10.1). There are two species:

(1) *Chlamydia trachomatis* which affects man,
(2) *Chlamydia psittaci* which mainly affects birds and animals, but occasionally infects man (see Table 10.2 for further details).

C. trachomatis causes eye infection in the newborn as well as in adults, and it can be found in the genital tract of the mothers of babies with such infection. Some patients with urethral gonorrhoea also harbour chlamydia; they often develop non-gonococcal urethritis which in this situation is called post-gonococcal urethritis. *C. trachomatis* also causes lymphogranuloma venereum. In the past there were difficulties distinguishing different strains of chlamydia, but recently rapid simple serotyping has been possible, using a microimmunofluorescent test (see Table 10.2). This test also

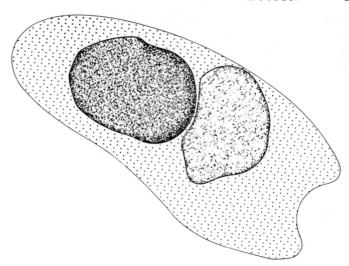

FIG. 10.1 *Chlamydia trachomatis* intracellular inclusion.

provides a rapid simple sensitive method for detecting antibodies in serum and other body fluids.

OTHER CAUSES OF NSU. *Ureaplasma urealyticum* can certainly cause urethritis, but how often it does so is not clear. The role of *Haemophilus vaginalis*, also called *Corynebacterium vaginale*, and recently *Gardnerella vaginalis*, is less clear.

TABLE. 10.2 Chlamydial diseases and serotypes.

Chlamydial Species	Disease	Serotypes
C. trachomatis	Hyperendemic trachoma. Inclusion conjunctivitis, NSGI. Lymphogranuloma venereum.	A, B, Ba, C. } D, E. F. G. H, I, J, K. L1, L11, L111
C. psittaci	Psittacosis in birds, Ornithosis in animals (occasionally infects man).	} Multiple.

Urinary infections. It is important to recognise the few cases of NSU due to upper urinary tract infection. Urinary symptoms with frequency are marked and in such cases urine culture (midstream urine—MSU) is mandatory. In these cases there may be underlying prostatitis or abnormality of the urinary tract.

Trichomonas vaginalis is sometimes found in the male partners of women with trichomoniasis. Trichomoniasis in men is commoner in Negroes than in whites.

Incubation period

This is commonly 2 or 3 weeks but may vary from a few days to 6 weeks.

Presentation and clinical features

Patients commonly present with:
    urethral discharge,
    burning on micturition.
The symptoms are milder than in gonococcal urethritis. Some patients are symptom free.

On examination, there is a mucoid or mucopurulent discharge, less profuse than in gonorrhoea, sometimes only apparent on gentle 'milking' or massage of the urethra. The meatal mucosa is rarely inflamed.

Mild cases may be recognised only after the patient has held his urine overnight and is examined and investigated the next morning before micturition.

Diagnosis

The clinical features of NSU can be confused with those of urethral gonorrhoea and a clinical diagnosis can *not* be made. Diagnosis depends on results of urethral investigations as outlined in Chapter 3.

The characteristic features are:
    presence of polymorphonuclear leucocytes in Gram-stained smears of urethral secretion in the absence of organisms and yeasts,

absence of trichomonads in a wet film of urethral secretion
mixed with saline.

These two findings lead to a rapid presumptive diagnosis of NSU in
the clinic. This should be supported by a negative result to a culture
for gonococci. Where facilities exist, a culture for chlamydia should
be taken.

The two-glass urine test shows:

changes in the first glass of urine,

clear urine in the second glass,

unless there is an underlying upper urinary tract infection when
there may be changes in the second glass.

If urethritis is suspected, for example where the patient has
symptoms but examination and investigation at the first visit are
negative, he must be told to hold his urine overnight as mentioned
above, and attend in the morning for further assessment.

Treatment

Antimicrobials. Treatment of NSU is less satisfactory than
treatment of gonorrhoea and syphilis. The most effective group of
drugs are the tetracyclines, though at present erythromycin stearate
seems to be equally useful. Both are effective against chlamydia,
but chlamydia-positive and chlamydia-negative urethritis respond
equally well. These antimicrobials appear to have their maximum
effect early in the course of the disease; later courses are less
effective. The optimum dose and duration is at present undecided,
but initially give:

oxytetracycline 250 mg four times a day for 14 days.

Ambulant patients have difficulty in remembering to take tablets
four times daily; useful alternatives are shown in Table 10.3.

General measures. Advise:

no sexual intercourse until antimicrobial therapy has been
completed, and response is satisfactory,

plenty of bland fluids so concentrated urine does not irritate the
urethra.

Alcohol is traditionally prohibited. The value of this measure
is not clear. In some patients alcohol consumption is followed by
urethral irritation though the relationship is obscure.

TABLE 10.3   Antimicrobial treatment of NSU.

Drug	Dose	Duration
Oxytetracycline	250 mg four times a day	14 Days.
Deteclo (triple tetracycline, Lederle)	1 tablet twice a day	14 Days.
Minocycline	100 mg twice a day	14 Days.
Erythromycin	250 mg four times a day	14 Days.
	500 mg twice a day	14 Days.

Some specialists consider 21 days treatment to be more effective.

Prognosis and cure rates

With the regimens outlined, cure rates are 80–85 per cent. It is often difficult to differentiate re-infection from treatment failure.

Follow-up after treatment

See Table 10.4.

Management of recurrence of NSU. The causes of recurrence of NSU are not clear, but consider the following:
    has the antimicrobial been taken as instructed?

TABLE 10.4   Follow-up of patients treated for NSU.

SEE
    On completing treatment,
    1–2 weeks after completing treatment,
    3 months after the start of treatment.

AT EACH VISIT
    Examine clinically,
    Investigate any discharge by Gram stain and microscopy for cells and organisms,
    Wet film for trichomonads,
    Culture for gonococci,
    Culture for other organisms where facilities allow,
    Two-glass urine test.

should another antimicrobial be considered or a longer course be prescribed?

have all relevant sexual contacts been treated?

is there any possibility of re-infection?

is the patient squeezing the urethra; this may delay or prevent healing?

has he a rare cause of urethritis such as trichomoniasis; commoner in Negroes?

has he prostatitis, urethral stricture or other urological disease?

Local complications

Any of the local complications described under gonococcal urethritis may occur though they are uncommon.

PROSTATITIS. *Acute prostatitis* is extremely rare.

Sub-acute prostatitis may be common with NSU but is usually symptomless and resolves with the urethritis. Recurrent NSU may lead to chronic prostatitis.

Chronic prostatitis may be symptomless, but may present with:
    pain:
        a dull perineal ache,
        penile tip pain,
        other pains,
    urinary symptoms:
        frequency,
        urgency,
        nocturia,
        mild obstructive symptoms,
        haematuria, usually mild,
        haemospermia,
    other symptoms:
        anxieties,
        obsession with symptoms,
    occasionally, generalised symptoms:
        fever,
        malaise.

Rectal examination may show:

> local or general tenderness of the prostate,
> nodularity,
> benign enlargement,
> a normal prostate.

The diagnosis can be made clinically if there is definite localised tenderness, or generalised tenderness (difficult to assess unless marked). In the absence of tenderness, gently massage the prostate, express prostatic secretion and examine it microscopically and by culture. On microscopy more than ten leucocytes per × 40 field or clumps of leucocytes are abnormal. In addition, arrange the following investigations:

> urine culture,
> urine cytology,
> intravenous urogram,
> cystourethroscopy.

Treatment of chronic prostatitis includes:

> high fluid intake,
> regular prostatic drainage,
> antimicrobials:
>> erythromycin 500 mg twice a day,
>> septrin 2 tablets twice a day,
>> minocycline 100 mg twice a day,
>> doxycycline 100 mg daily,
> continue for at least 1 month, and often for 3 months.

Non-specific proctitis

NSU occurs in homosexual men. Clinical and proctoscopic examination of their passive partners usually fails to show any symptoms or signs. Microscopy may or may not show leucocytes on Gram stains of rectal secretion. There is little information concerning chlamydia culture from the rectum. Thus recogntion of non-specific proctitis is controversial.

One solution to this problem is to examine contacts, investigate them by Gram stain of rectal secretion for leucocytes and organisms and culture for gonococci. Any conditions so discovered must be treated and in addition all contacts are given antimicrobial therapy such as:

> deteclo 1 tablet twice a day for 14 days.

Non-specific genital infection in women

NSU in men has most of the features of a sexually transmitted disease. For example:

> it occurs in the same age group as gonorrhoea,
>
> it is frequently associated with other STDs.

So far a corresponding clinical condition in women has not been identified apart from an occasional patient with a complication such as pelvic inflammatory disease (PID). In practice, recognition of uncomplicated non-specific genital infection (NSGI) can be made from the following:

> a positive chlamydia culture from the cervical secretion,
>
> a male partner with NSU.

Until chlamydia cultures become more widely available, the latter is probably the more usual criterion.

It is important to examine female partners of men with NSU, for other STDs may be found, such as trichomoniasis which may present as NSU in the male partner. In addition treatment prevents complications such as pelvic infections and eye infection in newborn babies.

Clinical features

Women with uncomplicated NSGI are often asymptomatic. When symptoms are present, they are usually mild and include:

> dysuria (burning on micturition),
>
> vaginal discharge (occasionally due to associated trichomoniasis),
>
> rarely marked dysuria plus frequency.

Examination commonly reveals no abnormality. Occasionally there may be:

> a cervical erosion with oedema and congestion,
>
> a mucopurulent cervical discharge,
>
> urethritis,
>
> proctitis.

None of these signs are diagnostic. Colposcopic examination of the cervix may show characteristic follicles similar to those seen in chlamydial infection of the eye. These follicles have also been observed in the rectal mucosa in chlamydial infection.

Investigation

It is important to undertake the routine genital investigations as outlined in Chapter 3. Gram stain of urethral secretion may show leucocytes which is unusual. Gram stain of cervical secretion may show a marked excess of leucocytes but this is difficult to interpret because cervical secretion contains leucocytes which vary in number with the phase of the menstrual cycle.

The vaginal secretion may also contain excess leucocytes.

No specific organisms are seen on microscopy or routine cultures for gonococci, trichomonads or candida.

The Papanicolaou-stained cervical smear may show excess leucocytes and inflammatory changes in the epithelial cells though these are non-specific, difficult to see, and their value is debatable.

Diagnosis of NSGI in women

As already stated, diagnosis usually rests on:

a positive chlamydia culture result,

a male partner with NSU.

The investigations outlined above provide useful additional information and reveal other STDs.

Treatment

Antimicrobial therapy. Give women the same treatment as men if the woman has no symptoms or signs and the routine Gram stains and cultures are normal. Antimicrobial treatment:

reduces the likelihood of complications,

prevents re-infection of the male partner.

Use the same antimicrobials as for the man with NSU as summarised in Table 10.5.

TABLE 10.5   Antimicrobial therapy for NSGI in women.

A	Oxytetracycline	250 mg four times a day for 14 days.
B	Deteclo (triple tetracycline, Lederle)	1 tablet twice a day for 14 days.
C	Minocycline	100 mg twice a day for 14 days.
D	Erythromycin stearate	250 mg four times a day for 14 days.
E	Erythromycin stearate	500 mg twice a day for 14 days.

Prescribe regimens B, C and E, for women who have difficulty in taking tablets four times a day.
Only give erythromycin stearate to pregnant women.

General measures. Advise against sexual intercourse until antimicrobial therapy has been completed and the male partner is responding satisfactorily.

Complications

Local. Any of the local complications which complicate gonorrhoea may complicate NSGI in women. The most important are:
  bartholinitis,
  salpingitis, or pelvic inflammatory disease (PID).

Bartholinitis presents with the same pain and swelling as gonococcal bartholinitis. There are various non-gonococcal causes of bartholinitis, including:
  chlamydia,
  bacteroides species,
  coliform bacillus.
All cases should be treated with aspiration as described under gonococcal bartholinitis. The aspirate should be sent to the laboratory for culture for bacteria and if possible chlamydia. Patients harbouring chlamydia, and women who are contacts of men with NSU should be treated with one of the regimens outlined in Table 10.5. In other cases, the choice of antimicrobial should be based on the results of sensitivity tests.

Pelvic inflammatory disease (PID) is more often non-gonococcal than gonococcal in origin. The presentation is similar to that of gonococcal PID. Again, the use of an IUD is associated with an increased risk of PID. The principles of treatment are:
  antimicrobials,
  rest.
In mild or moderate cases the antimicrobial regimens outlined in Table 10.5 suffices. In severe cases start with intravenous tetracycline and continue treatment for 21 days.

Chlamydial eye infection in the newborn. This is one of the most important complications of genital chlamydial infection. A mother harbouring genital chlamydia may infect her baby during parturition leading to:
  non-gonococcal ophthalmia neonatorum.
Chlamydial ophthalmia neonatorum is more common than

gonococcal ophthalmia and is only one cause of non-gonococcal ophthalmia neonatorum.

The incubation period is 5–14 days but may be shorter. The condition is usually milder than gonococcal ophthalmia but the two conditions may co-exist. Scarring and pannus may occur in apparently mild cases and the condition must be treated seriously.

Diagnosis ideally depends on:

    isolating chlamydia,

    in addition, take a swab for Gram stain from the eye; this will show leucocytes but no Gram negative diplococci,

    culture for gonococci, which is negative,

    culture for other micro-organisms,

    examine the mother and investigate as outlined,

    examine the father or the mother's recent sexual partners,

    NSU will usually be present.

Treatment of chlamydial and non-gonococcal ophthalmia, see Table 10.6.

TABLE 10.6   Treatment of non-gonococcal ophthalmia neonatorum.

Prescribe
    Chlortetracycline eye ointment,
    1% four times daily,
    Ensure mother applies it properly.
If response is unsatisfactory, give in addition:
    Erythromycin 30–40 mg/kg, in divided doses four times daily by mouth

---

Manage all cases in consultation with an ophthalmologist.

Neonatal chlamydial pneumonia. A few babies also develop pneumonia. This usually starts at the age of 2–3 weeks but is only usually diagnosed when the baby is aged 6 or more weeks.

    Features include:

    characteristic staccato cough,

    mucoid nasal discharge,

    diffuse infiltration and hyperinflation on the chest radiograph,

    C. trachomatis in nasopharyngeal secretion,

    antichlamydial serum antibodies detected by the micro IF test.

There is usually no fever.

Treatment is with erythromycin 30–40 mg kg, in four divided doses daily.

Chlamydial eye infection in adults is beyond the scope of this book. Recently, chlamydial pneumonia has been described in adults.

Generalised complications of chlamydial infection

The following have been reported:
   endocarditis,
   perihepatitis,
   febrile illness presenting as 'Pyrexia of Undetermined Origin (PUO)'.
Reiter's Disease is not strictly a complication of NSGI and is described in the next chapter.

Differential diagnosis

This is shown in Table 10.7.

TABLE 10.7 Differential diagnosis of non-specific genital infection.

Condition	Differential diagnosis
Non-specific urethritis	Urethral gonorrhoea (Chapter 8), Urinary infection,
Non-specific proctitis	Rectal gonorrhoea (Chapter 8), Proctitis due to other causes, Ischiorectal and related abscesses.
NSGI in women	Gonorrhoea (Chapter 8), Trichomoniasis (Chapter 12), Candidosis (Chapter 13), Urinary infection.
Non-gonococcal ophthalmia	Gonococcal ophthalmia (Chapter 8).

CHAPTER 11

Reiter's disease

This has a triad of main features:
    non-specific urethritis,
    arthritis,
    conjunctivitis.
It takes its name from a German, Hans Reiter, though it was described earlier by other physicians.

Prevalence

Approximately 1–3 per cent of men with NSU subsequently develop Reiter's disease, but probably many more cases are misdiagnosed. A few women appear to develop the syndrome but males predominate over females 15:1.

Aetiology

In Britain and North America the disease is associated with NSU. In other parts of the world it tends to follow:
    bacillary dysentery,
    amoebic dysentery,
    enteric disease,
    Yersinia infection,
    non-specific diarrhoea,
NSU is present in the dysenteric illness.

The nature of the association between NSU, diarrhoea, and the other features is not clear. Long-standing cases of Reiter's disease develop features indistinguishable from ankylosing spondylitis. The tissue typing antigen HLA B27, present in 95 per cent of patients with ankylosing condylitis, is found in 76 per cent of patients with Reiter's disease compared to only 9 per cent of patients with uncomplicted NSU. The significance of these associations is not clear.

Presentation and clinical features

COMMON PRESENTATIONS. The patients commonly present with:

NSU,

arthritis,

and perhaps conjunctivitis.

FULL CLINICAL FEATURES. The full clinical picture is summarised in Table 11.1.

TABLE 11.1   Clinical features of Reiter's disease.

NSU	Rarely
	    prostatitis,
	    cystitis.

Non-suppurative arthritis,	Usually polyarticular.

Conjunctivitis	Rarely
	    iritis,
	    corneal ulceration.

Circinate balanitis	Rounded erosions on glans penis.
Keratoderma blenorrhagica. Mouth ulcers. Rash	Especially on soles.

Rarely
    Cardiac disease, especially aortic regurgitation,
    Neurological disease,
    Pulmonary disease.	

NSU usually presents in the normal way. Occasionally it may be asymptomatic or the symptoms of prostatitis predominate. Urinary symptoms may be prominent but the NSU shows sterile pyuria indicating abacterial cystitis.

Arthritis. The joints affected in approximate descending order of frequency are:

knees,
ankles,
small joints of the feet,
upper limb joints,
back.

The joints of the lower limbs tend to be affected for longer than those of the upper limbs which may only be transiently involved. The arthritis is usually sub-acute with or without an effusion but occasionally it is acute. Backache is fairly common and there may be sacroiliitis. Temporomandibular and costochondral joints are occasionally involved.

Conjunctivitis is present in many cases but may be transient:
> it is usually bilateral,
> characteristically affects lateral tarsal conjunctivae of lower lids,
> occasionally, corneal ulceration complicates conjunctivitis,
> keratitis is rare,
> anterior uveitis usually appears late in the course of the disease and is associated with chronic sacroiliitis.

Circinate balanitis. In the uncircumcised, typical rounded erosions appear on the glans and underside of the prepuce; these may coalesce to form larger erosions with scalloped edges. In the circumcised, rounded red, raised, scaly lesions appear on the glans resembling those of the skin.

Erosions similar to those of circinate balanitis have been described on the vulva in women with other features of Reiter's disease.

Keratodermia blenorrhagica. The rash in Reiter's disease is more common in the venereal than in the dysenteric disease. The lesions usually start as dull red macules which develop into dry scaly thickened pustular-like lesions which commonly affect the soles where they may become extensive. Small, poorly developed lesions, sometimes just scaly macules, occur less commonly elsewhere on the body.

Mouth ulcers vary from aphthous-like ulcers to little patches of hyperaemia. in approximate descending order of frequency they occur on the:

    hard palate,
    soft palate,
    uvula,
    tongue,
    buccal mucosa.

Some lesions on the tongue are simply areas bare of normal papillae.

GENERAL FEATURES. At the beginning there is often:

    fever,
    malaise.

Patients with marked keratodermia often lose weight, occasionally severely.

RARE FEATURES include:

    cardiac disease,
        aortic regurgitation,
        myocarditis,
        pericarditis,
        conduction defects,
    neurological disease,
        peripheral neuritis,
        meningoencephalitis,
    pulmonary disease.

Investigations

Positive findings. While there are no specific investigations for this disease, the ESR is usually elevated, (up to 100 mm in the first hour).

There is slight neutrophil leucocytosis.

There may be mild normocytic anaemia.

The plasma proteins show a non-specific rise in alpha 2 globulin.

In the acute stage, radiographs of bones and joints may be normal, but:

    fluffy periostosis can appear early.

Later there may be:

    periostosis,
    osteoporosis,

erosions,
spurs at the attachment to the os calcis of:
>   plantar fascia,
>   Achilles tendon.

Lateral radiographs of the os calcis should be taken in all cases of suspected Reiter's disease.

Negative findings. It is important to exclude other causes of polyarthropathy by arranging the following investigations which should give negative results in all cases:
>   rheumatoid arthritis factor,
>   anti-nuclear factors,
>   serum uric acid,
>   anti-streptolysin 0 titre.

Diagnosis

This depends on:
>   clinical features, especially:
>>   urethritis,
>>   arthritis,
>>   conjunctivitis,
>   raised ESR,
>   negative results to investigations for other causes of polyarthropathy.

Treatment

This is summarised in Table 11.2.

In mild arthritis aspirin may suffice. In most cases an anti-inflammatory agent such as indomethacin is needed. In more severe cases light splints may help during the acute stage when rest is important. Admit severe cases to hospital. Once the acute stage is passed, the physiotherapist should start passive movements, and then gentle active movements as resolution proceeds. Aspirate moderate or large effusions.

If corneal ulceration or iritis develop, refer the patient to an ophthalmologist.

Consider systemic steroids in the patient with:
>   florid disease,
>   severe pain,

TABLE 11.2 Treatment of Reiter's disease.

Feature	Therapy
NSU	Antimicrobials as outlined in Chapter 10.
Arthritis	Rest at first, Physiotherapy later, Anti-inflammatory agents, such as Indomethacin 25–50 mg two or three times a day.
Conjunctivitis	Chloramphenicol eye drops.
Circinate balanitis	Usually saline washes, Occasionally, steroid cream as well.
Keratodermia blenorrhagia	Usually, simply keep clean, Occasionally, topical steroid cream
Mouth ulcers	Routine oral hygiene, Occasionally, corticosteroid lozenges.

wasting,
fever,
high ESR,

who is not responding to the measures outlined. Start with prednisone 40–60 mg daily in divided doses and reduce by 5 mg daily as soon as response is satisfactory.

When the dose is around 15–20 mg daily, then reduce more slowly, such as 5 mg every 2–4 weeks. A problem with systemic corticosteroids is that response may be poor but the condition worsens when the dose is reduced. There is no way of predicting cases with a good or bad response.

It is important to remember that the disease as seen in Britain and North America is usually associated with sexually-acquired NSU. Management involves contact tracing.

Prognosis

The first attack lasts for a mean of 3 months. Patients motivated towards rapid recovery improve sooner than those not so motivated.

The condition tends to recur and such recurrence may be precipitated by freshly-acquired NSU. Patients should be warned of this danger and advised to report the first suggestion of NSU as early treatment may prevent a recurrence of Reiter's disease.

The course of the syndrome may be:
  recurrent attacks without residual damage to joints,
  painful deformities of the feet including:
      plantar and Achilles tendon spurs,
      pes planus,
      multiple hammer toe deformities,
  spondylitis with:
      polyarthritis especially of ankles and feet,
      later spinal stiffness with comparatively little pain,
      sacroiliitis, often progressive,
  ultimately, joint changes indistinguishable from classical
      ankylosing spondylitis, often with:
            anterior uveitis,
            prostatitis,
            seminal vesiculitis.

Differential diagnosis

Distinguish Reiter's disease from:
      rheumatoid arthritis,
      ankylosing spondylitis,
      psoriatic arthritis,
      gonococcal arthritis (p. 116),
      other causes of acute pyogenic arthritis,
      gout,
      acute rheumatic fever,
      systemic lupus erythematosis,
      anterior uveitis due to other causes,
      Behçet's syndrome (p. 225),
      Stevens–Johnson syndrome (p. 227).

CHAPTER 12

Trichomoniasis

Aetiology

Trichomoniasis is caused by the flagellate parasite *Trichomonas vaginalis* (Fig. 12.1) which, despite its name, is found in various sites including:

FIG. 12.1   *Trichomonas vaginalis.*

149

vagina,
urethra in both males and females,
occasionally the bladder.

The organism varies in size from that of a pus cell to two and a half times that size.

Prevalence

T. vaginalis is second only to candidosis as the cause of vaginal discharge. In contrast, the parasite is rarely recognised in the male. It appears to be more common in Negroes than in whites.

Trichomoniasis in the female

Infestation in the female is more often found during the period of greater sexual activity, between 18 and 35 years, than in older or younger women. It is nearly always sexually acquired. It often occurs with gonorrhoea, especially in Negro women.

Incubation period

This is probably 4 days to 3 weeks.

Common presentation and clinical features

The vagina is involved in most cases. The patients complain of:
vaginal discharge:
thin,
yellow,
offensive.
vulvovaginal irritation or pain,
dysuria (usually external),
dyspareunia.
On examination, there may be:
vaginal discharge:
thin,
yellow,
perhaps frothy.
Reddening of the mucosa of:
vulva,

vagina,
cervix,
which may be marked.

Note, however, that vaginal trichomoniasis can be present *without* symptoms or signs.

Urethral trichomoniasis is present in up to half of the cases of vaginal infestation. This causes:
internal dysuria,
frequency if the trigone of the bladder is involved.
There is some doubt if the cervix and upper genital tract is involved.
Skenitis and bartholinitis are rare.

Investigations and diagnosis

Clinical findings must be supported by laboratory investigations as described in Chapter 3, to establish the diagnosis. Essentially the investigations are:
secretion from the posterior vaginal fornix,
mixed with saline and immediately examined under the microscope,
inoculated into trichomonas culture medium,
T. vaginalis can also be recognised in Papanicoloaou-stained cervical smears.

Microscopic examination of fresh, wet smears and of cultures after incubation shows the morphology and motility, namely active movement of the flagellae and undulating membrane, and when very active, the flagellae actually jerk the parasites about with a characteristic movement.

Wet smears, cultures and Papanicolaou-stained cervical smears give equally good results, but the best results are obtained by using all three methods together.

Treatment and cure rates

The most widely used preparation is metronidazole (Flagyl). Alternatives are nimorazole (Naxogin) or tinidazole (Fasigyn). Both are taken orally. See Table 12.1 for doses.

During pregnancy, avoid these preparations which may just possibly be teratogenic during the first trimester and use clotrimazole pessaries, 1×100 mg pessary at night for 6 nights. Give

TABLE 12.1   Treatment of trichomoniasis.

Drug	Dosage	Cure rate (%)
Metronidazole	200 mg three times a day for 7 days	98
	400 mg twice a day for 5 days	98
	2 g in a single dose	98
Nimorazole	250 mg twice a day for 6 days	90
	1 g daily for 3 days	90
	2 g in a single dose	90
Tinidazole	250 mg three times a day for 7 days	90
	2 g in a single dose	95

metronidazole 200 mg three times a day for 7 days or 400 mg twice a day for 5 days during later pregnancy.

An important part of the treatment is to examine sexual partners and prescribe the same treatment even if the organism is not found. This avoids the risk of re-infection.

Follow-up

This is outlined in Table 12.2.

In the event of recurrence, try to differentiate re-infection from treatment failure. In the former case, repeat the original treatment and trace the contact, in the latter:

increase the dose, or
prolong the course, or
change the drug.

TABLE 12.2   Follow-up after treatment of vaginal trichomoniasis.

SEE
1 week after start of treatment,
2 weeks after start of treatment
3 months after start of treatment.

AT EACH VISIT
Examine clinically,
Repeat smears and cultures for trichomonads.

AT FIRST VISIT
Repeat investigations for gonorrhoea.

Complications

Local complications are rare. There may be:
    skenitis,
    bartholinitis,
    salpingitis (possibly).
Systemic spread is not recognised.

Differential diagnosis

The main condition to differentiate is vulvovaginal candidosis
(Chapter 13). Other conditions are shown in Table 12.3.

TABLE 12.3   Other causes of vaginal discharge.

INCREASED BUT NORMAL VAGINAL SECRETION
    At ovulation and before menstruation,
    During sexual excitement,
    During pregnancy.
ABNORMAL DISCHARGE
Non-infective causes
    Chemical irritants such as douches, deodorants,
    Mechanical irritants such as foreign bodies, trauma,
    Degenerative conditions such as senile vaginitis.
Infective causes (other than yeasts and trichomonads)
    Bacteria such as *Haemophilus* or *Gardnerella vaginalis*,
    Parasites such as threadworms,
    Protozoa such as amoebae.
NOTE Vaginal discharge may arise from disease of
    Bartholin's glands,
    Skene's ducts,
    Cervix,
    Uterus.

Trichomoniasis in the male

Urethral infestation is rarely recognised in men and is more
common in Negroes than in whites though the reasons for this are
not known. *T. vaginalis* produces a low-grade urethritis.
Trichomonal balanitis is also occasionally seen, again usually in
Negroes.

Incubation period

This is usually 4 days to 3 weeks.

Common presentation and clinical features of trichomonal urethritis

The patient may complain of:
mild discharge,
mild dysuria.
There may be no symptoms. On examination, there may be:
a slight clear or grey urethral discharge,
usually there is no meatal inflammation,
often there is no discharge.

Investigations and diagnosis

As in the female, the diagnosis must be based on identifying the parasite by means of the investigations described in Chapter 3.

Briefly, insert a bacteriological loop, 1–2 cm into the urethra and gently scrape the mucosa. Examine the secretion so obtained under the microscope. In addition, inoculate secretion into trichomonal culture medium. Note the trichomonads must be identified to make the diagnosis.

In addition, examine the urine by the two-glass test. Characteristically, the first glass contains little comma-shaped specks. In suspected cases such as contacts, centrifuge the urine in the first glass and examine the deposit by microscopy and culture. Sometimes these patients have urethral or meatal stenosis.

Treatment

As in the female.

Follow-up

See 1–2 weeks and 3 months after the start of treatment and repeat any positive investigations.

Complications

The only local complications of urethritis usually recognised are:

prostatitis (rare),
epididymitis (very rare).
The former can be diagnosed from the presence of trichomonads in the prostatic fluid. The latter must be inferred from clinical epididymitis in association with proven trichomonal urethritis or prostatitis.

Differential diagnosis

Differentiate trichomonal urethritis from:
gonococcal urethritis,
non-gonococcal urethritis.
Differentiate trichomonal from other causes of prostatitis.

Trichomonal balanitis

This is usually a moist or erosive balanitis, diagnosed by finding trichomonads in the exudate on microscopy or culture (Chapter 3). Treat as already outlined. Repeat the investigations afterwards to ensure cure. Differentiate from balanitis due to other causes: notably yeasts (Chapters 13 and 17).

Candidosis

This is also called candidiasis, the older name was moniliasis, while the colloquial name is thrush. The main genital manifestations are:
    vaginitis in women,
    balanitis or balanoposthitis in men.

Aetiology

Most cases are due to the yeast-like fungus called *Candida albicans*: the old name was *Monilia albicans*. For other causes see Table 13.1.

TABLE 13.1   Causes of candidosis.

C. albicans	81%
Torulopsis glabrata	16%
Other yeasts	3%

Strictly, the terms candidosis and candidal should be reserved for cases in which the causative organism has been fully identified, and the term yeast infection used for other cases. The terms are frequently used loosely as if they had the same meaning and this is continued here.

It is not clear if *C. albicans* or other yeasts are normal inhabitants of the vagina and the sub-preputial space. Yeasts are certainly normal inhabitants of the mouth and gut. Not all cases of genital candidosis are sexually transmitted: yeasts can readily spread from anus to vulva and vagina. Once established in or on the genitals, they can be transmitted sexually; an asymptomatic partner can be the source of repeated re-infection.

Presdisposing factors. These include:
    diabetes mellitus,
    pregnancy,
    broad-spectrum antimicrobials,
    oral contraceptives,
    corticosteroid drugs,
    immunosuppressive drugs,
    iron deficiency anaemia.

Probably, yeasts can be tolerated as commensals in the absence of predisposing factors or in the presence of only one factor. Symptomatic disease may only appear when two or more factors act together.

Prevalence

Yeasts are the most common identifiable cause of vaginitis or vaginal discharge and they are a common cause of balanitis and balanoposthitis.

Candidosis in women

Women may harbour yeasts in the vagina and on the vulva without symptoms or signs.

Incubation period

This is difficult to determine as it is frequently not clear when the yeasts reached the genitals.

Presentation and clinical features

The usual presentation is:
    vulvovaginal itch or irritation which may be worse pre-
        menstrually,
    vaginal discharge.
There may be:
    dysuria (external),
    dyspareunia.
    The dysuria is due to urine flowing over the inflamed vulva.

On examination, the following signs may be present:
   on the vulva:
      slight oedema,
      slight redness,
      white discharge,
      fissures,
   in the vagina:
      white discharge adhering in lumps to vaginal walls and
        cervix (like cottage cheese).
There may be:
   no symptoms,
   no signs.

Investigations

Collect exudate from the lateral vaginal walls and Gram stain and examine microscopically for yeast forms (Fig. 13.1). Culture the exudate on Sabouraud's dextrose agar medium. Test the urine for sugar.

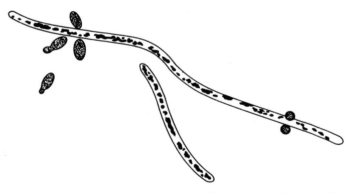

FIG. 13.1   Yeast showing pseudomycelium, spores and yeast cells.

Diagnosis

This depends on:
   clinical features, if any,
   more especially, on results of mycological investigations.

Treatment

Only local antifungal agents are currently available and fully evaluated but results of treatment are unsatisfactory. The principles of treatment are to:

apply topical antifungal agents to affected surfaces long
   enough to be effective,
avoid re-infection from a sexual partner,
prevent auto-infection from the bowel.

In addition, keeping the vulva cool and dry probably helps. This is achieved by:

careful hygiene, especially thorough drying,
cotton, rather than synthetic, underwear.

The basis of treatment is intravaginal pessaries or cream inserted high into the vagina at night; these should be prescribed for all cases, see Table 13.2 for details.

TABLE 13.2   Antifungal pessaries for vaginal candidosis.

Drug	Strength of pessary	Dose	Duration
Nystatin	100,000 units	2 at night	14 nights
Clotrimazole	100 mg	1 at night	6 nights
Clotrimazole	200 mg	1 at night	3 nights
Miconazole	100 mg	1 twice daily	7 nights
Econazole	150 mg	1 at night	3 nights
Nystavescent	100,000 units	2 at night	14 nights

Advise all patients to avoid intercourse until cure has been
   established.

If there are vulval symptoms or signs:
   advise saline washes twice a day followed by:
      antifungal cream:
         nystatin,
         clotrimazole,
         miconazole.

Advise all patients to avoid intercourse until cure has been established.

Prognosis

Cure rates from 65–90 per cent have been reported after initial treatment. In cases failing to respond to treatment consider:
1. failure to use treatment correctly,
2. auto-infection,
3. re-infection,
4. predisposing factors as already listed.

Re-treatment. Consider the following:
longer course of the original pessaries,
a different vaginal preparation,
vulval cream,
nystatin tablets (500,000 international units) 1 four times a day for 14 days, little nystatin is absorbed from the bowel; oral therapy acts by reducing bowel carriage and preventing auto-infection.

Follow-up

See at the intervals described in Table 13.3.

TABLE   13.3 Follow-up   of   vaginal candidosis.

SEE
1–2 weeks after start of therapy,
4 weeks after start of therapy,
3 months after start of therapy.

AT EACH VISIT
Examine,
Repeat Gram stain and culture for yeasts.

Complications

Theoretically, systemic spread can occur. This is usually only found in severely ill patients taking:
corticosteroids,
immunosuppressives,
broad spectrum antimicrobials.

It is likely that in such patients vulvovaginal candidosis is part of a more generalised candidosis.

Differential diagnosis

The main condition to differentiate is trichomoniasis. Other conditions are shown in Table 13.4.

TABLE 13.4 Other causes of vaginal discharge.

INCREASED BUT NORMAL VAGINAL SECRETION
    At ovulation and before menstruation,
    During sexual excitement,
    During pregnancy.

ABNORMAL DISCHARGE
Non-infective causes
    Chemical irritants such as douches, deodorants,
    Mechanical irritants such as foreign bodies, trauma,
    Degenerative conditions such as senile vaginitis.
Infective causes (other than yeasts and trichomonads)
    Bacteria such as *Haemophilus,* or *Gardnerella vaginalis,*
    Parasites such as threadworms,
    Protozoa such as amoebae.
NOTE Vaginal discharge may arise from disease of:
    Bartholin's glands,
        Skene's ducts,
        Cervix,
        Uterus.

Candidosis in men

Yeasts are carried equally often by circumcised and uncircumcised men but the latter are more likely to develop symptoms. Approximately half of the male contacts of women with candidosis harbour the organism: most female contacts of men with candidosis harbour the organisms. Genital yeasts in men:
    may be present without symptoms or signs,
    may cause balanitis,
    rarely cause urethritis.

Incubation period

Men may develop symptoms almost immediately after intercourse.

Initially, these symptoms may be due to trauma; symptoms starting soon after intercourse may also be due to a hypersensitivity reaction.

Presentation and clinical features

Circumcised and uncircumcised men may carry yeasts without any symptoms or signs.

Balanitis and balanoposthitis cause:
irritation, burning, or itching subpreputially or on glans,
redness, subpreputially or on glans,
difficulty in retracting prepuce,
subpreputial discharge.

Mild urethritis often occurs with balanitis. The patients may complain of:
slight urethral discharge,
mild dysuria.
On examination, the following signs may be present:
patchy white exudate,
red patches on glans and underside of prepuce,
little vesicles,
erosions,
fissures at tip of prepuce,
prepuce tight and difficult to retract,
no abnormal sign may be present.

Investigations

A swab should be taken of the exudate if present. If not, the swab should be rolled around the coronal sulcus. A smear and culture should be made as described in Chapter 3. The Gram stain shows Gram positive:
pseudomycelium,
spores,
yeast cells (Fig. 13.1).
Cultures on Sabouraud's dextrose agar are more sensitive.

Yeast forms and pseudomycelium may be recognisable on the wet-film preparations used for microscopic identification of *T. vaginalis* but these films should not be relied on to identify yeasts.

In candidal urethritis, the exudate contains yeast forms and epithelial cells with comparatively few leucocytes.

Test the urine for sugar in all cases.

Diagnosis

This depends on:
clinical features, if any,
results of mycological investigations.

As far as possible, the diagnosis should be based on the mycological investigations.

Treatment

Balanitis and balanoposthitis. Clean thoroughly with saline, then bathe with saline for 5–10 minutes, two or three times daily. Then apply one of the creams listed in Table 13.5. Continue treatment for 2 weeks even if clinical response is satisfactory before this. In cases responding more slowly, it is good practice to continue therapy for at least a week after all symptoms and signs have gone.

TABLE 13.5 Treatment of candidal balanitis and balanoposthitis.

Saline washing and bathing, followed by:
Nystatin cream,
Clotrimazole cream,
Miconazole cream.

Urethritis. Instil nystatin suspension 100,000 international units per ml twice daily for 14 days or amphotercin 3 per cent lotion twice daily for 14 days.

Prognosis

Most cases respond satisfactorily.
In cases failing to respond, consider:
1. failure to follow treatment correctly,
2. further sexual contact,
3. the predisposing factors already listed.

For re-treatment, consider:
1. longer use of the original preparation,
2. another preparation.

Follow-up

See Table 13.6.

TABLE 13.6   Follow-up after treatment for candidal balanitis.

SEE
2 weeks after start of therapy,
4 weeks after start of therapy,
3 months after start of therapy.

AT EACH VISIT
Examine clinically,
Repeat Gram stain and culture.

NOTE
If response is satisfactory, omit visit at 4 weeks.

Complications

Systemic spread can theoretically occur but even in patients on corticosteroids or immunosuppressives, systemic spread from candidal balanitis is improbable. In such patients candidal balanitis is more likely to be part of a generalised candidosis.

Phimosis may also occur. Treat with saline washouts using a soft plastic catheter plus instillation of nystatin. All such patients must be advised to have a circumcision.

Differential diagnosis

See Table 13.7.

Crural candidosis

In men, an erythematous, confluent, macular rash may develop in the crural region. It is sometimes itchy. In addition to the

TABLE 13.7 Differential diagnosis of candidal balanitis.

Trichomonal balanitis (Chapter 12),
Balanitis due to other microorganisms (Chapter 17),
Circinate balanitis in Reiter's disease (Chapter 11),
Hypersensitivity reaction to an organism in vagina,
Toxic or hypersensitivity reaction to:
    Contraceptive creams,
    Antiseptics,
    Rubber sheath,
    Vaginal cap,
    Chemicals in sheath or cap.

---

predisposing factors already mentioned, in this condition remember:
    poor hygiene,
    obesity.

This condition is one form of cutaneous candidosis. See page 231 for clinical features and management.

Anal and perianal candidosis

As yeasts are normal inhabitants of the bowel, they contaminate the anus. Usually they cause no trouble, but they occasionally cause a skin reaction with:
    itch,
    redness,
    white soggy skin,
    linear cracks.

In addition to the predisposing factors already mentioned, remember:
    diarrhoea,
    trauma from toilet paper and other causes,
    poor hygiene,
    obesity.

Investigations and diagnosis

It is important to differentiate anal candidosis from other causes of pruritis ani. Take a swab from the affected area for a Gram-stained smear and culture on Sabouraud's medium. The diagnosis should be based on the clinical appearance and the results of these investigations. Test the urine for sugar.

Treatment

Wash carefully,
bathe with saline,
dry thoroughly,
apply clotrimazole cream.
As in crural candidosis, it may be wise to prescribe hydrocortisone cream as well.
Again, there are advantages in wearing loose cotton clothing.

Differential diagnosis

Differentiate from other causes of pruritis ani, including:
threadworms,
haemorrhoids.

CHAPTER 14

Sexually transmitted viral conditions

Genital and ano-rectal herpes simplex infection

Aetiology

The common oral herpes simplex infection (usually in the form of cold sores on the lips) is usually due to Type I herpes simplex virus (HSV). Genital and anorectal infection is usually due to the antigenically different Type II HSV. The primary attack of Type I HSV infection is often during childhood and is sub-clinical.

Primary infection by either virus in later life may produce a more severe illness. After the primary infection with either type of virus, some individuals suffer mild recurrent episodes of clinical disease. Between clinical attacks, the virus lies dormant in the posterior nerve root ganglia. The virus is acquired by contact and with anogenital infection this is usually sexual contact. Occasionally, Type I virus is found in anogenital infection and Type II in oral infection.

Incidence

Genital herpes simplex virus is the most common identifiable cause of genital ulceration. In Britain, seven cases of genital herpes simplex infection are reported for every one case of primary syphilis. The incidence is rising and in 1979, 9500 cases were reported by STD clinics in England.

Incubation period

This is usually 4–5 days.

Common presentation

This is genital ulceration. In the common recurrent episode, there is a cluster of erosions. In the rarer primary attack, the erosions are more widespread.

Primary genital herpes. This is characterised by:
>   prodromal discomfort,
>   genital vesicles,
>   genital erosions,
>   inguinal adenopathy,
>   cervicitis.

In addition, there may be:
>   malaise,
>   fever,
>   urinary retention.

In men, vesicles and erosions may be:
>   on or near the penis,
>   there may be urethritis.

In women, the lesions may be:
>   on or near the vulva,
>   on the cervix.

Cervical involvement includes:
>   a normal looking cervix, but herpes virus can be cultured from the cervical os,
>   a so-called cervical erosion (culture for herpes virus positive),
>   herpetic vesicles and erosions on the cervix,
>   acute necrotic cervicitis (which has a characteristic white appearance).

Vesicles are a few mm in diameter and soon rupture leaving erosions with a narrow bright red margin. Secondary bacterial infection may develop leading to vesicopustules or infected erosions.

The inguinal nodes are usually slightly to moderately enlarged, may be tender, but do not suppurate. Occasionally a finger is infected. Urinary retention may occur due to:
>   pain from urine flowing over erosions in and near the terminal urethra,
>   direct involvement of sacral nerves and spinal cord.

The lesions of the primary attack take 2–4 weeks to heal. In the longer attacks, vesicles appear in crops so vesicles, pustules and erosions are seen together.

Primary anorectal herpes. This occurs in homosexuals. Features include:

    anal vesicles,
    anal erosions,
    proctitis,
    constipation,
    sacral nerve root pains (S2 to S4),
    as in genital disease, the vesicles soon rupture.

The proctitis appears as a general marked redness, sometimes with a purulent exudate. Constipation develops for the same reasons as urinary retention.

Recurrent genital herpes. The main features are:

    localised prodromal discomfort,
    cluster of vesicles,
    cluster of erosions (Fig. 14.1),

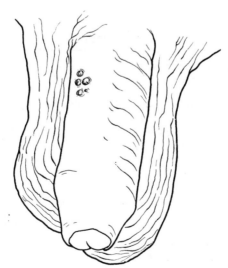

FIG. 14.1 A typical cluster of recurrent erosions in genital herpes simplex.

They usually occur:
>   on or near the external genitalia,
>   occasionally, the Type II virus also produces lesions:
>>   on a finger,
>>   on the lips,
>>   in the mouth.

Vesicles are present for a short time, perhaps only a few hours, before they rupture leaving the erosions which have the same appearance as in the primary attack. Recurrent lesions may heal in 2–5 days but occasionally take as long as 10 days. Scarring is rare but may follow secondary infection.

It is not clear why some patients suffer recurrent attacks of genital herpes or what precipitates recurrence. Some patients have frequent recurrences leading to great misery.

Recurrent anal herpes. This produces clusters of vesicles and erosions similar to those seen in recurrent genital herpes.

Investigations

These are summarised in Table 14.1.

TABLE 14.1 Investigation of suspected anogenital herpes simplex infection.

SPECIFIC INVESTIGATIONS
>   Viral culture from:
>>   vesicle fluid,
>>   scrapings from fresh erosions (within 3 days in recurrence and within 5 days in a primary attack).
>   Cervical cytology smear,
>   Serum antibody tests:
>>   in acute and convalescent sera,
>>   in a suspected primary attack.

OTHER INVESTIGATIONS
>   Dark ground examinations from erosions,
>   Blood for serological tests (VDRL and TPHA) from all cases,
>   Consider investigations for:
>>   Chancroid,
>>   Granuloma inguinale,
>>   Lymphogranuloma venereum,
>   if a patient or contact have recently visited the Tropics.

Herpes simplex virus can be readily cultured from swabs placed in Hank's medium for transport to the laboratory.

Whenever a culture is taken from a genital lesion in the female, take another swab from the cervical os.

Cervical herpes virus infection can produce cytological change on cervical smears (Fig. 14.2), though virus can be shed from the cervix without cytological change.

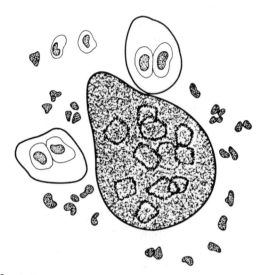

FIG. 14.2 A Papanicolaou-stained cervical smear showing infected multinucleate giant cell in genital herpes simplex.

Clinical suspicion of a primary attack can be supported by a rise in serum antibody titre measured by the herpes simplex virus complement fixation test (HSVCFT) in acute phase serum taken on presentation and a (convalescent) sample collected 2 or 3 weeks later. If the patient presents late there may be a fall in titre between the first and second samples. Recurrent infections are not usually associated with significant change in serum HSVCFT titre.

Diagnosis

This is based on clinical appearance. Viral cultures and antibody results provide confirmation.

Treatment

General measures. Treatment must take into account the natural history of herpes infection. As stated above, recurrent herpes heals in 10 days and primary disease in 2–4 weeks provided there is no secondary infection. All that is required is to keep the lesions clean with saline. If secondary infection does occur, give:

> sulphadimidine 1 g three times a day for 7 days, or
> co-trimoxazole 2 tabs twice a day for 7 days.

Avoid treponemacidal antimicrobials which may confuse the diagnosis of co-incidental syphilis.

Root pains occasionally need analgesics. Constipated bowel action returns to normal without treatment. In urinary retention, encourage the patient to urinate while in a hot bath; avoid catheterisation if at all possible.

Antiviral agents. *Idoxuridine* is the most widely used. This is available as a 5 per cent solution in the organic solvent dimethylsulphoxide (DMSO), but it is painful to apply and expensive. Higher concentrations have been used but there is no convincing evidence of their benefit. Idoxuridine is only of use if started within the first 2–3 days of a recurrent attack or the first 5 days of a primary attack. Apply four times daily for a maximum of 4 days.

Acycloguanosine is a new antiviral agent which is highly active against herpes simplex virus *in vitro*. It has given good preliminary results as a topical application in genital herpes, but these await confirmation. It may prove safe for systemic administration; a much more attractive therapeutic proposition for a virus that lies dormant in nerve root ganglia.

Prognosis

All attacks heal, usually within the time periods mentioned. Treatment merely:

> reduces the duration of virus shedding,
> hastens healing,
> reduces the duration of symptoms.

Follow-up

If virus cultures are positive and there is no suggestion of concomitant syphilis, once healing is complete see 3 months after the onset.

If there is any suggestion of syphilis, see every 2–4 weeks for 3 months. At each visit:

examine clinically,

repeat serological tests (VDRL and TPHA),

take swabs for viral culture from any fresh lesions.

Complications

Newborn infants. These may be infected during parturition from herpes virus in the cervix. When herpes infection is suspected in the mother, repeated viral cultures should be taken in late pregnancy (for example, weekly during the last 1–2 months). If these prove positive, some obstetricians consider elective Caesarian section is indicated. The baby is specially at risk from primary infection in the mother for there is no protective maternal antibody to cross the placenta as there is in recurrent attacks.

Systemic complications. These may occur in primary attacks, including:

hepatitis,

myelitis,

encephalitis which tends to follow Type I infection,

meningitis which tends to follow Type II infection.

Carcinoma of the cervix. There is an association between herpes simplex virus infection of the cervix and subsequent carcinoma, but the nature of this association is at present not known. This is why the cervical os is cultured at the same time as any lesions elsewhere. All women with positive cervical culture should be advised to have an annual cervical Papanicolaou smear.

Differential diagnosis

See Table 14.2.

TABLE 14.2 Differential diagnosis of genital herpes simplex.

VESICULAR STAGE
    Herpes zoster,
    Vaccinia (rarely).

EROSIVE STAGE
    In patients with no recent connection with the Tropics:
        Primary syphilis,
        Secondary syphilis,
        Erosive balanitis,
        Trauma,
        Scabies.
    Less commonly:
        Vincent's ulceration,
        Orogenital ulceration,
        Behcet's syndrome,
        Stevens–Johnson syndrome,
        Gumma.
    In patients with recent connection with the Tropics:
        Chancroid,
        Granuloma inguinale,
        Lymphogranuloma venereum,
        Tuberculosis.

Genital warts

This section covers:
    genital warts,
    anorectal warts.
Anorectal warts are more common in homosexual men than heterosexual men, but they do appear in apparently exclusively heterosexual men; they also occur in women, usually by backwards spread from the vulva.

Aetiology

These warts are due to a DNA Papova virus which is transferred by person to person contact. Anogenital wart virus resembles the virus of skin warts.

Incidence

The incidence of warts is increasing in Britain at present. Warts are more common than genital herpes simplex infection but less common than gonorrhoea. Total cases of warts reported by STD clinics in 1979 in England was 27,600.

Incubation period

This varies from 3 weeks to about 8 months but has a mean of about 3 months.

Presentation and clinical features

A man with genital warts usually sees them. A woman with genital warts may feel an itch or feel the warts; anal warts present in the same way.

The age of onset of genital warts is similar to that of gonorrhoea and is later than the age when skin warts appear on the hands.

On the cold, dry areas of the genitals, warts start as small flat lesions 1–2 mm in diameter, they resemble skin warts, grow slowly, but usually remain flat. In warm moist areas they are filiform and larger, varying in diameter from 1 to about 5 mm. Larger warts may be pedunculated, are occasionally several cm in diameter and may resemble a cauliflower in appearance. Growth is favoured by warmth and moisture, especially by:

vaginal discharge,
sub-preputial discharge,
rectal discharge,
pregnancy,
poor hygiene.

Larger warts appear under the prepuce (Fig. 14.3) than on the uncircumcised penis. Anal warts can be massive. Warts appearing or enlarging during pregnancy often resolve after delivery.

Warts appear on sites traumatised during intercourse so tend to occur in the same places as the primary chancre of syphilis as shown in Table 14.3.

Investigations and diagnosis

The diagnosis of warts is usually based on clinical appearance. Biopsy is rarely needed for confirmation, but must be undertaken if there is any suggestion of malignancy such as undue hardness in consistency.

FIG. 14.3   Sub-preputial warts.

TABLE 14.3   Sites of warts in approximate descending order of frequency.

IN MEN
    Coronal sulcus,
    Fraenum,
    Glans,
    Prepuce,
    Meatus,
    Shaft.

IN WOMEN
    Fourchette,
    Elsewhere on the vulva,
    Vaginal walls,
    Cervix, occasionally,
    Perineum.

IN MEN AND WOMEN
    Anus,
    Rectum,
    Mouth, rarely.

Vaginal warts usually only appear with vulval warts; they tend to extend along the vagina from the vulva.

It is, as usual, important to exclude other STDs and in particular to exclude all possible causes of:
    vaginal discharge,
    sub-preputial discharge,
    rectal discharge.

Whenever anal warts are seen, a proctoscope must be passed and the lower rectum inspected for warts and excess secretion, and a swab taken for Gram stain and culture for gonococci.

Treatment

This may be prolonged but is important, for warts, being sexually transmitted, spread if left untreated, and they are unsightly. General and specific measures are indicated.

General measures. These include:
> keep the affected parts:
>> clean,
>> cool,
>> dry,
>
> exclude or treat causes of excess discharge outlined above,
> contact tracing,
> sheath *must* be worn if intercourse takes place before resolution is complete.

Specific measures

These are listed in Table 14.4.

TABLE 14.4   Treatment of warts.

Podophyllin 5–25%
Trichloaracetic acid 50–100%
Electrocautery,
Cryosurgery,
Scissor excision.

Podophyllin, a cytotoxic agent, can be diluted in various solvents including surgical spirit and compound tincture of benzoin. It is a cytotoxic agent which may irritate normal skin and mucous membrane. Begin treatment with a 10 per cent concentration, limit the paint to the warts themselves and advise careful washing after 4 hours. If this procedure is tolerated, gradually increase strength and duration to 25 per cent concentration for 24 hours. Several applications once or twice a week may be necessary.

Trichloracetic acid: use if podophyllin is ineffective after a few weeks. This has a caustic action, so limit application to the wart itself. It is more effective than podophyllin for hyperkeratotic skin warts on the penile shaft and meatal warts.

Electrocautery is performed under local (LA) or general anaesthesia (GA). Reserve it for:

> extensive warts and use under GA,
>
> isolated warts resistant to other measures and used with LA.

Cryosurgery has so far been less widely used than electrocautery, but appears to give similar results. It has the advantages that:

> additional anaesthesia is unnecessary,
>
> it is easier to control.

Scissor excision has so far only been used for anorectal warts, and under GA. It is particularly useful for extensive warts for it leaves less scarring.

Consider circumcision when an uncircumcised man has persistent or recurrent warts under the prepuce.

Only consider treating warts during pregnancy if they are so large that they may cause mechanical difficulty during delivery. Choice of treatment should rest with the obstetrician.

Side effects: Large amounts of podophyllin may cause:

> peripheral neuropathy,
>
> stillbirth.

Trichloracetic acid may cause:

> caustic burns.

Prognosis and follow-up

Warts may:

> persist,
>
> recur,
>
> resolve spontaneously.

Review patients 2–3 months after all warts have disappeared to ensure cure. Little firm information is available concerning the relative value of different forms of therapy.

Complications

These include:

> benign giant penile warts,
>
> malignant change.

Benign giant penile warts are called Buschke–Lowenstein tumours. Malignant change very rarely occurs in these lesions or ordinary genital and anal warts.

Differential diagnosis

See Table 14.5.

TABLE 14.5 Differential diagnosis of anogenital warts.

Differentiate from
    Condylomata lata,
    Molluscum contagiosum,
    Carcinoma,
    Pearly penile papules—keratoangioma,
    Sebaceous cysts.

In most cases, the clinical appearance of these conditions is characteristic. If in doubt, especially when suspecting nodular carcinoma, arrange a biopsy.

Molluscum contagiosum

Aetiology

This condition is due to a pox virus.

Prevalence

It is comparatively rare in STD clinics in Britain at present. Only 1000 cases were reported in 1979.

Incubation period

This is from 3 weeks to several months.

Presentation and clinical features

Pink or white shiny wax-like papules develop, each with a central pit filled with a white plug. They occur on the penis, scrotum and vulva, and elsewhere on the skin. Secondary infection may lead to pustule formation.

Investigations and diagnosis

Diagnosis usually rests on the clinical appearance.

The contents of the papule can be expressed, smeared on a slide and stained by Giemsa's method when large swollen 'balloon' cells can be seen which contain viral inclusions.

Other STDs must be excluded in the usual ways.

Treatment

Express the contents.
Cauterise the base with:
pure phenol,
electrocautery.

Differential diagnosis

Differentiate from:
warts,
sebaceous cysts.

Hepatitis

Hepatitis occurs in a number of viral conditions including those produced by Epstein–Barr virus, cytomegalovirus, herpes simplex virus and togavirus (yellow fever). There are also at least three forms of the condition which appear to be due to hepatitis virus, mainly:
hepatitis A (previously called infective hepatitis),
hepatitis B (previously called serum or syringe transmitted hepatitis),
and in addition there is so-called:
non-A non-B hepatitis.

Hepatitis B is sexually transmitted among homosexuals. It has been more extensively studied than hepatitis A which may also be sexually transmitted among homosexuals. The epidemiology of these diseases among homosexuals is considered on pages 14 and 250.

Hepatitis B

Aetiology

Hepatitis B is due to a virus (HBV) which only replicates in the liver. Antigens including surface antigen (HBsAg) and e antigen (HBeAg) can be detected in blood and blood products. HBeAg is a marker of infectivity. Transmission via blood and blood products can occur, hence the old name of serum or syringe transmitted hepatitis. Although the exact mode of sexual transmission is not clear, available evidence indicates that it is related to the trauma of sexual intercourse. While sexual transmission among male homosexuals is now the main method of spread in the West, in the Third World spread is from mother to baby.

Clinical features

Serum hepatitis used to present with jaundice which had a long incubation period of 2–3 months. Sexually-transmitted hepatitis B may also have an incubation period of 2–3 months. It rarely presents with jaundice and in Britain and the rest of the Western World it is more likely to be detected as a result of screening of homosexuals for HBsAg. A few have, or have had, mild symptoms of hepatitis but frank jaundice is rare. Serum liver function tests show about 60 per cent of HBsAg carriers have mildly abnormal results. Liver biopsies have been performed on comparatively few of such cases, but half have shown chronic active hepatitis or active cirrhosis.

Diagnosis

This depends on finding HBsAg in the serum.

Treatment

At present there is no effective treatment. A vaccine is at present under trial and preliminary results are encouraging. In the meantime, warn all HBsAg carriers of their potential infectivity and advise minimal partner change. Examine all possible sexual contacts. Homosexuals should have regular checks for HBsAg carriage.

Prognosis

Patients infected with hepatitis B virus may develop circulating antibody (anti-HBs) which is protective and circulating antigens disappear. As indicated above, others develop cirrhosis and in a few patients this progresses rapidly to death.

Complications

A sub-group of male homosexual carriers has been identified with the following characteristics:

persistent high titre of HBsAg antigen,

abnormal liver function tests without jaundice,

HBeAg–e antigen; a marker of infectivity.

These patients are potent sources of infection and should be strongly urged to minimise partner change.

Hepatitis A

This was formerly called infective hepatitis, it has a shorter incubation period than hepatitis B and spreads by the faecal—oral route. An antigen can be detected by a radioimmune assay (RIA), rising titres of serum antibodies can be demonstrated, or specific IgM class antibody may be found in convalescent sera. Like hepatitis B it appears to be more commonly sexually transmitted in homosexuals than in heterosexuals. Hepatitis A is usually symptomless; when there are symptoms they are mild and frank jaundice is rare. Serum liver function tests are usually only mildly abnormal. The disease is self-limiting.

Non-A non-B hepatitis

When there is no adequate laboratory evidence of hepatitis A or B, or the other viruses mentioned above, hepatitis may be called non-A non-B hepatitis; this may be due to one or more viruses.

Herpes zoster (shingles)

Invasion of the dorsal root ganglia of the sacral nerve roots supplying the genitals by the varicella zoster virus is a rare occurence that can cause herpes zoster or shingles affecting the genitals. This has similar features affecting other dorsal root ganglia. The virus can lie dormant in the ganglia for long periods.

Aetiology

The clinical condition is due to reactivation of varicella zoster virus; the cause of reactivation is usually unknown but may occur in association with the depressed immunocompetence found with:

reticuloses,
leukaemia,
tumours,

while sometimes, reactivation follows trauma. The condition is rarely diagnosed in STD clinics.

Presentation and clinical features

The patient usually presents with vesicles and erosions.

The condition usually starts with pain in the distribution of the affected nerve root. After 3 or 4 days, the skin in the affected areas becomes red, vesicles appear and after a further 3 or 4 days, they dry up unless secondary infection supervenes in which case they persist longer. They often heal with slight scarring. The lesions are limited to one side.

Investigations and diagnosis

The diagnosis is based on the clinical features; they are characteristic but as this is a rare condition it is sometimes forgotten. A clinical diagnosis can be supported by the demonstration of characteristic virus particles by electron microscopy and can be confirmed by virus culture from the lesion.

If only erosions are present it is important to exclude syphilis and herpes simplex. It is also important to exclude the underlying conditions listed above.

Treatment

Idoxuridine, adenine, arabinoside, and acycloguanosine have all been recommended for local application but their value is questionable. In the meantime a good regimen is:

keep lesions clean with saline,

treat secondary infection with:

sulphadimidine 1 g three times a day for 7 days, or

co-trimoxazole 2 tablets twice a day for 7 days.

Complications

Post-herpetic neuralgia is rare.

Differential diagnosis

See Table 14.6.

TABLE 14.6 Differential diagnosis of genital herpes zoster.

Vesicular stage	Herpes simplex, Vaccinia (rare).
Erosive stage (patient having no recent connection with Tropics)	Primary syphilis, Secondary syphilis, Erosive balanitis, Herpes simplex, Trauma, Scabies.
Uncommonly	Carcinoma, Vincent's ulceration, Orogenital ulceration: Behçet's syndrome, Stevens–Johnson syndrome, Gumma.
Erosive stage (where there is a recent connection with the Tropics)	Chancroid, Granuloma inguinale, Lymphogranuloma venereum, Tuberculosis.

Cytomegalovirus disease

Cytomegalovirus (CMV) can be transmitted sexually and infection is usually asymptomatic but the virus can produce a disease in adults like glandular fever (Epstein–Barr virus mononucleosis) in which the Paul–Bunnell test is negative.

The virus can cross the placenta producing congenital infection. Infection in debilitated immunosuppressed patients may produce a terminal illness, often with pneumonia, but almost any organ may be affected.

Aetiology

The cytomegalovirus is one of the herpes group of viruses.

CMV disease in young adults

Prevalence

Sixty to seventy per cent of pregnant women have serum antibodies when they first attend the antenatal clinic. A few women (1–4 per cent) develop primary infection during pregnancy. Congenital infection develops in 0 5–3 per cent of populations in different parts of the world.

Clinical features

Most young adults have asymptomatic infection. Those with symptoms complain of:
> headache,
> backache,
> abdominal pain,
> sore throat.

On examination there may be:
> pharyngitis,
> hepatosplenomegaly.

Sometimes:
> jaundice,
> polyneuritis.

Investigations

These inlude:
> virus isolation from urine, saliva, liver and other organs,
> rising titre of CMV antibodies,
> lymphocytosis with atypical lymphocytes,
> abnormal liver function tests,

thrombocytopenia,
evidence of myocarditis and pericarditis,
negative findings to tests for Epstein–Barr virus.

Diagnosis

This depends on the clinical picture, plus a rising titre of anti-CMV antibodies.

Treatment

There is no specific treatment.

Complications

The most important complications are:
congenital infection,
pneumonia.

Differential diagnosis

Differentiate from:
Epstein–Barr virus mononucleosis,
hepatitis due to other causes, such as hepatitis B.

Congenital CMV disease—cytomegalic inclusion disease in the newborn

Ninety-five per cent are symptom and sign free.
Those who develop the clinical features of cytomegalic inclusion disease of the newborn have:
jaundice,
hepatosplenomegaly,
microcephaly,
encephalitis,
choroidoretinitis,
pneumonia,
rash.

Investigations

These include:
    virus isolation from urine and saliva,
    the presence of specific IgM antibody,
    lymphocytosis with atypical lymphocytes,
    abnormal liver function tests,
    evidence of haemolytic anaemia.

Diagnosis

Diagnosis is based on:
    clinical picture, plus:
        virus isolation, or
        presence of specific IgM antibody.

Treatment

There is no specific treatment. Live CMV vaccines are being studied.

Complications

These include:
    sensorineural deafness,
    mental retardation.

Differential diagnosis

Differentiate cytomegalic inclusion disease from conditions such as rubella, toxoplasmosis, and herpes simplex infection.

CHAPTER 15

Parasitic infestations

Scabies

Aetiology

Scabies is due to the mite *Sarcoptes scabiei*. Infestation usually occurs as a result of close bodily contact. Among adults this usually occurs during sexual contact, but spread can occur to other family members especially among those who sleep in the same bed.

Prevalence

The prevalence of scabies in Britain is fairly steady, 2391 cases were reported from STD clinics in 1979.

Incubation period

In the first attack the incubation period is 3–6 weeks. If there is a subsequent attack the incubation period is very much shorter and may only be 24 hours.

Presentation

The patient classically presents with:
> itch at night and when warm during the day,
> rash.

Other clinical features

The typical rash consists of greyish–white elongated burrows in the webs between fingers and toes. Around the time itching starts erythema appears around the burrows. Scratching, abrasion and secondary infection often follow. Genital lesions are dusky red papules surrounded by erythema (Fig. 15.1). The burrows may be seen curled up within the papules. Scratching leads to excoriation and crusting. The lesions are seen on the scrotum, prepuce and shaft of the penis.

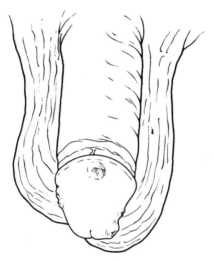

FIG. 15.1   Typical papular lesions in genital scabies.

They are rarely seen on the female genitalia.

Burrows may be more widely distributed and there may be little erythematous papules on the anterior aspects of the wrists, the posterior aspect of the elbows, the anterior axillary folds, the breasts in the female, around the waist and on the buttocks. Sensitisation may lead to dry eczema and sometimes urticaria. The head is spared except in infants. Secondary bacterial infection is common in neglected cases with impetigo and boils.

Investigation and diagnosis

The mite can be seen in scrapings from a burrow, mixed with potassium hydroxide and examined under a microscope using low power magnification.

The diagnosis is usually based on:
    history of itch,
    clinical appearance.

Treatment

Apply one of the following:
    benzyl benzoate (25 per cent) emulsion,
    gamma benzene hexachloride (1 per cent) lotion,
    malathion (0·5 per cent) lotion.

With benzyl benzoate and gamma benzene hexachloride advise the following regime:

1. bath,
2. apply lotion all over the body from neck downwards,
3. wait 24 hours,
4. repeat bath and application as in 1 and 2,
5. wait 24 hours,
6. repeat bath,
7. change underclothes, night attire and bed linen; ordinary laundering suffices.

It is important that:
    the patient has an assistant,
    the *whole* body is covered from the neck down,
    there is no washing, even of the hands, apart from the three baths mentioned above.

Most patients find gamma benzene hexachloride less irritating than benzyl benzoate. Warn the patient that symptoms take a week or two to resolve and not to repeat treatment any more or dermatitis will develop, especially with benzyl benzoate.

Apply malathion once; experience of this is limited and it can be dangerously inflammable.

In all cases:
    examine sexual contacts and treat as necessary,
    examine members of the family and treat as necessary.

Prognosis

Most cases respond satisfactorily. In the remainder, consider:
    has the treatment been used properly?
    is recurrence due to re-infection?
    retreat cautiously to avoid dermatitis.

Follow-up

See:

> 1 week after treatment,
> 6 weeks after treatment,
> 3 months after treatment.

At each visit:

> examine,
> repeat antitreponemal antibody tests.

If there is no suggestion of syphilis, the visit at 6 weeks may be omitted.

Differential diagnosis

See Table 15.1.

TABLE 15.1   Differential diagnosis of scabies.

Itchy conditions such as:
Pediculosis,
Urticaria,
Prurigo,
Lichen planus,
Lichen simplex,
Reticulosis.

Pubic lice or pediculosis pubis

Aetiology

This condition is due to *Phthirus pubis* or the pubic louse. It is similar to *Pediculosis capitis* (head louse) and to *Pediculosis corporis* (body louse). The public louse has a shorter tail and does not move about as much as the other two parasites. The mature form is transferred during body contact which in adults usually occurs during sexual contact. The louse may be deposited in other hairy areas of the body than the pubic hair.

Incidence

The incidence of pubic lice is gradually increasing. It is more common that scabies with 8272 cases reported from STD clinics in 1979 in Britain.

Incubation period

The patient complains of itch when the adult louse buries its mouth parts in the skin to feed. If a large crop of adults are acquired and start to feed, symptoms start at once.

Presentation

The patient either:
>   complains of itch,
>   notices the crab-like adult (Fig. 15.2).

FIG. 15.2   Phthirus pubis.

Clinical features

The adult female lays eggs at the base of a hair, they adhere to the hair by a chitinous envelope or nit (Fig. 15.3). As the hair grows the nit moves further away from the skin. After about a week, the egg hatches into a miniature form which descends to the base of the hair where it remains as a non-descript brownish-speck 1–3 mm in diameter before maturing after about another week. The adult is

FIG. 15.3 A nit.

also brownish and is about 2 mm in diameter. Although called pediculosis pubis, the parasite may be seen in:

pubic hair,
body hair,
and occasionally in the eyebrows and eyelashes.

Diagnosis

This is made on the history and clinical appearance. Examine suspicious areas with a hand lens. If in doubt, remove suspicious pediculi and inspect under the low power of the microscope.

Treatment

Rub either:

gamma benzene hydrochloride 1 per cent, or
benzyl benzoate application 25 per cent

into all the hairy areas on the body including apparently non-infested areas; there may be newlaid eggs too small to see. One application is usually enough.

In heavy infestation, repeat after 3 days.

Good results are also obtained with one application of 0 5 per cent malathion.

Shaving is not indicated with these remedies.

Examine sexual contacts and family members and treat as necessary.

Prognosis

Most cases respond satisfactorily to the above regimens.

Follow-up

This is similar to the follow-up for scabies, see page 191.

Differential diagnosis

See Table 15.2.

TABLE 15.2   Differential diagnosis of pediculosis pubis.

Differentiate from:
Flea infestation,
Eczema,
Neurodermatitis.

CHAPTER 16

Sexually transmitted diseases more commonly seen in hot climates

The conditions considered in this chapter are:
  chancroid or soft sore,
  granuloma inguinale or donovanosis,
  lymphogranuloma venereum.
These conditions are common in hot, mainly tropical climates, but with air travel, patients may present with these conditions anywhere in the world. Furthermore, a patient may have had contact with a partner who has recently returned from the tropics.

In the past, confusion was caused by other names given to granuloma inguinale and lymphogranuloma venereum.

Chancroid

Chancroid is characterised by:
  genital ulceration,
  inguinal buboes (enlarged lymph nodes).
There is a tendency to regard all non-syphilitic genital ulcers as chancroid, but this is a specific condition. It is more common among the poor and dirty, and is rare where good hygiene prevails.

Aetiology

Chancroid is due to the small Gram-negative bacillus *Haemophilus ducreyi*. Strictly, the diagnosis should only be made when this organism is identified.

Prevalence

Chancroid is more common in:
>   tropical Africa,
>   South America,
>   the Far East.

It is probably wise to consider this diagnosis in anyone who is:
>   in the tropics,
>   recently back from the tropics, or
>   who has had a contact, in or recently returned from, a
>   tropical or sub-tropical area.

Incubation period

This is short, usually 1–8 days, rarely longer.

Common presentation and clinical features

Common presentation. Multiple painful genital ulcers and inguinal buboes.

Clinical features. Lesions start as painful, tender papules which soon become pustules and break down to form shallow ulcers (Fig. 16.1). The characteristics of the ulcers are shown in Table 16.1.

Inguinal lymph nodes enlarge in half the cases within a week of onset. They are firm, tender and matted together (adherent).

Investigations

Always exclude syphilis by means of at least three dark-ground examinations on consecutive days and serological tests repeated over 3 months. Remember primary syphilis and chancroid may occur together. Primary syphilis and chancroid are both common in many tropical areas.

Specific tests. See Table 16.2

Gram stain. Clean the ulcer carefully with saline, scrape material from the edge or aspirate pus from a bubo. Make a smear and stain by Gram's method.

H. ducreyi may often be seen arranged in chains, giving the

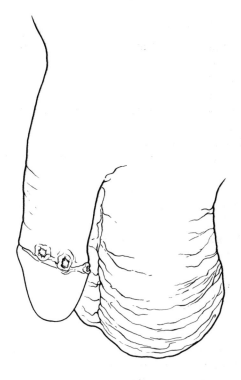

FIG. 16.1   Mutiple ragged ulcers in chancroid.

TABLE 16.1   Characteristics of chancroidal ulceration.

Numbers	Usually multiple, Occasionally single.
Shape	Circular or oval.
Margin	Red, Ragged, Undermined.
Base	Granulation tissue, Slough often covers base.
Pain/tenderness	Usually very painful and tender Occasionally relatively painless and non-tender.
Induration	None.

TABLE 16.2   Specific investigations
for chancroid

Gram stain,
Culture,
Biopsy and histology,
Skin test.

appearance of a 'school of fish' (Fig. 16.2). It is often difficult to
recognise *H. ducreyi* among the secondary organisms.

Culture. Special media are required which include fresh blood. In
the past rabbit's blood was used but recently a medium using the
patient's own blood has apparently given good results.

Biopsy. Although the histology is not specific, some authorities
regard biopsy as the most accurate diagnostic method. The
following features have been described:

superficial necrosis,
occasional necrosis in deeper layers,
pallisading and endothelial proliferation of blood vessels,
occasional thrombosis,
infiltration with:

polymorphonuclear leucocytes,
plasma cells,
lymphocytes.

H. Ducreyi may be seen.

FIG. 16.2   *Haemophilus ducreyi* in chancroid.

Skin tests. An antigen preparation with killed *H. ducreyi* in suspension was used as an intradermal test but is now considered to give too many inaccurate results and has been abandoned.

Diagnosis

This depends on the clinical appearance and positive results to at least one of the diagnostic tests.

Treatment

As in all cases of genital ulceration, avoid antitreponemal therapy while dark ground examinations for *T. pallidum* are being done. Avoid antitreponemal antimicrobials altogether.

Local treatment. Careful cleaning and bathing with saline is all that is required.

Antimicrobial therapy. Use the drugs listed in Table 16.3.

TABLE 16.3   Antimicrobial therapy for chancroid.

Sulphadimidine	2 g orally at once, then 1 g 6-hourly for 7–14 days.
Co-trimoxazole	2 tablets twice a day orally for 7–10 days.
Streptomycin	1 g intramuscularly daily for 7–14 days.
Oxytetracycline	500 mg 6-hourly orally for 10–20 days.

Sulphadimidine has the advantage of economy and is the drug of first choice.
Better results may be obtained with streptomycin if given with sulphadimidine.
Oxytetracycline is antitreponemal, so only use if other antimicrobials fail.

Prognosis

Most of the drugs mentioned have given failures in one or more parts of the world. A change of antimicrobial nearly always produces healing.

Follow-up

All cases must be followed for 3 months in case co-incidental syphilis is initially missed. A good routine is to see patients:
    monthly for 3 months.
  At each visit:
    examine clinically,
    take blood for serological tests (VDRL and TPHA).

Complications

These include:
    lymph node suppuration,
    phimosis,
    paraphimosis,
    phagedenal tissue destruction,
    extragenital lesions.

Lymph node suppuration may lead to softening and fluctuation with the formation of a unilocular abscess. The overlying skin becomes shiny, tense, red and hot. The abscess may point and burst producing a sinus and spreading ulceration. When an abscess is suspected, aspirate, repeatedly if necessary; do not incise or a sinus forms and is very slow to heal.

Phimosis or paraphimosis may complicate lesions of the prepuce. A dorsal slit may be required.

Phagedena is probably related to secondary infection, often with Vincent's organisms. Occasionally, tissue destruction is dramatic, giving rise to remarkable loss of penile tissue and dramatic widespread ulceration. The myth that venereal disease can destroy the penis probably arose from phagedena.

Extragenital lesions have occasionally been reported. They may be more common than is realised as this diagnosis may not be considered.

Differential diagnosis

See Tables 16.4 and 16.5.

Granuloma inguinale

Granuloma inguinale is characterised by a large genital lesion. The disease is sexually transmitted but is not very contagious.

TABLE 16.4 Differential diagnosis of chancroidal ulcers.

Differentiate ulcers from:

MORE COMMON CONDITIONS
Primary syphilis (Chapter 4),
Secondary syphilis (Chapter 4),
Herpes simplex (Chapter 14),
Erosive balanitis (Chapter 17),
Trauma (Chapter 17),
Lymphogranuloma venereum (LGV),
Granuloma inguinale.

LESS COMMON CONDITIONS
Herpes zoster (Chapter 14),
Carcinoma (Chapter 17),
Vincent's angina (Chapter 17),
Orogenital ulceration
Stevens–Johnson syndrome (Chapter 17),
Behçet's syndrome (Chapter 17)
Gumma (Chapter 6),
Tuberculosis (Chapter 17).

TABLE 16.5 Differential diagnosis of inguinal lymph node enlargement.

NON-SUPPURATIVE ENLARGEMENT
Primary syphilis (Chapter 4),
Secondary syphilis (Chapter 4),
Primary herpes simplex (Chapter 14),
Carcinoma,
Reticulosis,
Leukaemia.

SUPPURATIVE ENLARGEMENT
Chancroid,
Lymphogranuloma venereum,
Pyogenic infection of lesions in genitals and nearby, including anus,
Infection of lower limbs,
Tuberculosis,
Cat scratch disease.

Aetiology

Granuloma inguinale is due to an organism called *Donovania granulomatis* or Donovan's body (or occasionally, *Calymmatobacterium granulomatis*). It is a Gram-negative curved bacillus, though also described as ovoid, and capsulated and non-capsulated forms are seen (Fig. 16.3). It requires special media for growth in the laboratory.

FIG. 16.3   Donovan's body, usually seen in clusters, in granuloma inguinale.

Prevalence

Granuloma inguinale occurs almost exclusively in coloured people, is on the whole uncommon, but is found in tropical and sub-tropical areas and this diagnosis should be considered in anyone:

in these areas,
recently returned from these areas,
who has had contact in or recently returned from, a tropical or sub-tropical area.

It is more common in:

Southern India,
Papua New Guinea,
Central and West Africa,
West Indies,
Southern USA,
South America.

Incubation period

This is not accurately established but appears to vary from a few days to about 2 months.

Common presentation and clinical features

Common presentation. This is a granulomatous genital ulcer.

Clinical features. The lesions start as painless papules which progress to form spreading granulomatous ulcers with characteristic rolled edges. The base of the lesions is usually clean and may vary in colour from pale pink to deep red, while the surface has a soft velvety appearance. Lesions start on the external genitalia (Fig. 16.4) but may spread widely and involve the surrounding skin.

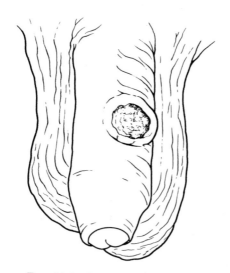

FIG. 16.4   Granuloma inguinale.

Subcutaneous granulomas may develop in the inguinal region and these may be mistaken for inguinal adenopathy. They may break down producing granulomatous ulcers. Secondary infection may supervene and be associated with inguinal adenopathy.

Investigations

Donovan's bodies can be identified in scrapings from the margin of an ulcer stained by Giemsa's method and in biopsy specimens stained by Wright's, Giemsa's, or Leishman's method. Histological examination of biopsies also aids the diagnosis and assists in differentiating from:

> lymphogranuloma venereum,
> carcinoma,
> exclude syphilis by means of repeated dark ground examinations and serological tests.

Diagnosis

This depends on:

> the clinical appearance,
> recognition of Donovan's bodies,

or failing that;

> the histological appearance.

Treatment and prognosis

Again, avoid antitreponemal therapy, at least until dark-ground examinations have been done.

Local saline bathing suffices.

Antimicrobial therapy. See Table 16.6.

TABLE 16.6   Antimicrobial treatment of granuloma inguinale.

Streptomycin	1 g twice a day i.m. for 10–20 days, 1 g four times a day i.m. for 5 days.
Oxytetracycline	500 mg 6-hourly orally for 14–21 days.
In addition, the following drugs have been reported to be effective:	
Co-trimoxazole	2 tablets twice a day orally for 10 days.
Gentamicin	1 mg/kg three times a day for 8–12 days.
Most cases respond satisfactorily to streptomycin or tetracycline.	

Follow-up

Again, to ensure that there is no co-incidental syphilis:

> see monthly for 3 months.

At each visit:
 examine clinically,
 take blood for serological tests (VDRL and TPHA).

Complications

Untreated lesions gradually enlarge and may involve the:
 rectum, especially in women,
 surrounding skin.
 Fibrosis during healing may lead to:
  tissue distortion,
  elephantiasis.
Neoplastic change may develop in long-standing cases.
Extra-genital lesions have been reported, affecting:
 face,
 neck,
 mouth,
 throat,
 bones,
 joints.

Differential diagnosis

In early cases, consider the conditions mentioned in Table 16.4 (replacing granuloma inguinale with chancroid). In addition, consider:
 amoebiasis,
 schistosomiasis.

Lymphogranuloma venereum

Lymphogranuloma venereum (LGV) is characterised by:
 an insignificant genital lesion,
 inguinal buboes.

Aetiology

LGV is due to *Chlamydia trachomatis* (Fig. 16.5), serotypes L1, L11, and L111.

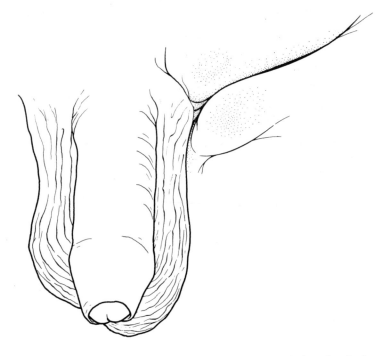

FIG. 16.5 Lymph node enlargement above and below inguinal ligament, producing the 'sign of the groove' in lymphogranuloma venereum.

Prevalence

LGV is mainly found in countries with warm climates. It appears to be more common in men than in women.

Incubation period

This is probably about 4–35 days, although longer periods have been reported.

Common presentation and clinical features

LGV has a wide variety of clinical features. One common presentation is an inguinal bubo.

Primary genital lesion

This is usually a single vesicle or papule,
it may ulcerate; maximum diameter 6 mm,
it is painless and non-indurated,
the patient may describe it as a 'pimple',
the patient may not notice it, hence the difficulty in
    determining the incubation period.

Inguinal adenopathy (or inguinal syndrome). This starts between 4
days and 4 months after the primary lesion. Involvement is
unilateral in two-thirds of cases. Lymph nodes are initially:

firm,
only slightly painful.

As the disease progresses:

lymph node swelling increases,
nodes mat together,
they adhere to the skin,
overlying skin becomes a dusky red,
softening and fluctuation develop,
multiple abscesses may form,
nodes enlarge above and below the inguinal ligament which
    produces a groove: the so-called 'sign of the groove'
nodes may enlarge up to and over the pelvic brim,
perforation of buboes may produce multiple sinuses,
involvement of pelvic nodes may produce abdominal pain,
proctoscopy may reveal proctitis which is more common in
    women.

Constitutional symptoms may develop during this stage and may
dominate the clinical picture. They include:

fever,
malaise,
anorexia,
nausea,
vomiting,
variable macular rash,
hepatosplenomegaly.

These symptoms may be more common in some parts of the world,
such as the Far East, than in others.

Later manifestations. These include:

scarring,

genital syndrome,
anorectal syndrome.
Scarring in the inguinal regions may be helpful in the diagnosis of the other later manifestations.

Genital elephantiasis. Destruction and distortion of lymphatic drainage leads to:
  genital elephantiasis (esthiomene) due to lymphoedema (only mild or moderate and never as dramatic as in filariasis),
  vegitations and polypoidal growths,
  occasional elephantiasis of one leg.
There may also be:
  multiple fistulae:
          rectal,
          vaginal,
          urinary.
  non-gonococcal urethritis,
  destructive ulceration,
  healing with fibrosis may lead to distortion, e.g. of penis.
These changes are all more common in Negroes.
  Anorectal syndrome. The main features are:
  proctitis,
  rectal stricture,
  rectal ulcerations,
  rectal fistulae,
  perirectal abscesses.
These features are more common in women than in men. Blood, mucus and pus are passed per rectum. The mucosa of the anorectum may be rough with a characteristic surface on digital examination resembling morocco leather. The changes tend to be most severe 5 cm from the anal margin. A stricture may develop a few months to 10 years later; it may be very short or extend up to 20 cm.

Investigations

When the primary genital lesion is present, it is again important to exclude syphilis by taking:
        dark-ground examinations for *T. pallidum* daily for at least three days,
        blood for serological tests (VDRL and TPHA) at once and repeating monthly for 3 months.

Specific investigations. See Table 16.7.

TABLE 16.7 Investigations for suspected LGV.

Stage	Investigation
Primary genital lesion	Swab from lesion to culture for *C. trachomatis*, *C. trachomatis* micro IF[1] antibody tests.
Inguinal adenopathy	Culture pus for *C. trachomatis*, *C. trachomatis* micro IF test.
Later manifestations	Culture pus for *C. trachomatis*, *C. trachomatis* micro IF[1] test, Biopsy and histology.

N.B.: Remember investigations to exclude syphilis.
[1]Micro IF: Microimmunofluorescence.

The micro IF test can be used to type chlamydia. The micro IF test may show a rising serum antibody titre in the stages of the primary genital lesion or inguinal adenopathy. Thereafter, sustained high antibody titres strongly indicate LGV and confirm a clinical diagnosis.

An alternative to the micro IF test is the lymphogranuloma venereum complement fixation test (LGVCFT). This uses a psittacosis antigen and gives false-positive and false-negative results. A fourfold rise in titre during the primary genital lesion or inguinal adenopathy is a strong indication of LGV and supports a clinical diagnosis.

Another technique was the intradermal Frei test, which involved intradermal injection of antigen from organisms grown in egg yolk cultures. It gave even less reliable results than the LGVCFT, so has been abandoned.

Diagnosis

This depends on the:
    clinical picture,
    isolation of *C. trachomatis* sero-type L1, L11, or L111, or high or rising titres of serum antibodies,
    biopsy and histology in the later stages.

Treatment

This includes:
    antimicrobial therapy,
    other measures.

Antimicrobial therapy. The antimicrobials which may be used
include:
    sulphadimidine,
    co-trimoxazole,
    tetracycline,
    erythromycin,
    rifampicin.
Sulphadimidine and Co-trimoxazole probably only control
secondary infection. They may be prescribed during the early stage
when syphilis is being excluded.

Oxytetracycline is the drug of choice for definitive treatment. The
dosage and duration varies with the stage and severity of the
disease. Response may also vary with the part of the world in which
the disease is contracted. For example, LGV contracted in the Far
East may need larger doses than when it is contracted in India.

In severely ill patients with the inguinal syndrome, give
oxytetracycline 1 g orally, 6-hourly until all constitutional
symptoms settle. Continue with 500 mg 6-hourly for 2–3 weeks.
Finally, give 250 mg 6-hourly to complete 4–6 weeks therapy in all.

Milder, earlier cases may only require oxytetracycline 500 mg
6-hourly for 14 days.

It is worthwhile treating early cases energetically to try to prevent
the severe later manifestations. In the later stages, treat as in the
severe early cases.

Erythromycin. Give erythromycin stearate 500 mg orally, 6-
hourly for 14 days, continue with 250 mg 6-hourly to complete 4
weeks therapy if needed.

Rifampicin. Because of its importance in the treatment of
tuberculosis, keep rifampicin in reserve for cases not responding to
oxytetracycline or erythromycin.

Other measures.

Bed rest is important for the acutely ill patient.

Buboes. Aspirate, if necessary repeatedly; do not incise or a sinus
forms which is very slow to heal.

Surgery has proved disappointing but must be considered for:
abscesses,
fistulae,
strictures.

Prognosis

With energetic antimicrobial treatment, cases with inguinal adenopathy respond well and late lesions are few and mild.

The prognosis for the later manifestations is unsatisfactory even with prolonged energetic antimicrobial treatment.

Follow-up

In the early stages:
see monthly for 3 months after the start of therapy,
at each visit; examine and take blood for serological tests (VDRL and TPHA).
In the late stages, prolonged follow-up may be necessary to avoid problems from complications.

Complications

The main complications are:
rectal obstruction,
neoplastic change.

Differential diagnosis

In the stage of the primary genital lesion, consider the conditions mentioned in Table 16.4 (replacing LGV with chancroid). During the inguinal syndrome, consider the conditions listed in Table 16.5.

In cases with marked febrile symptoms, consider all the conditions included in the diagnosis of 'pyrexia of undetermined origin'.

In the later stages, consider the following conditions:
filariasis,
actinomycosis,
amoebiasis,
schistisomiasis,
malignancy,
Hodgkin's disease,
inflammatory bowel disease.

CHAPTER 17

Other genital conditions

Ulcers and related conditions

Balanitis and balanoposthitis

Balanitis is inflammation of the glans.

Posthitis is inflammation of the preputial mucosa.

Balanoposthitis is inflammation of the glans and prepuce but the term balanitis is often used 'loosely' when balanoposthitis is the correct term.

Aetiology

In Britain, yeasts, especially *Candida albicans*, are the most common cause of balanitis, but there are other causes. Furthermore, predisposing conditions may be present.

Predisposing conditions include:

    poor hygiene,
    long prepuce,
    tight prepuce,
    trauma,
    diabetes mellitus,
    antiseptics,
    hypersensitivity, for example to:
        drugs,
        contraceptives.

As this list suggests, some cases of balanitis are not sexually transmitted.

Infective causes:

    Yeasts, especially *Candida albicans*,

212

Trichomonas vaginalis,
Vincent's organisms,
streptococci,
anaerobic bacteria.
Balanitis may also occur in association with:
syphilis,
chancroid,
gonorrhoea,
herpes simplex.
Special forms of balanitis include:
circinate balanitis in Reiter's Disease (Chapter 11),
balanitis xerotica obliterans,
plasma cell balanitis of Zoon.

Clinical features

See Table 17.1.

TABLE 17.1   Clinical features of balanoposthitis.

SYMPTOMS
Spots, rash, redness,
Itch, discomfort, pain,
Discharge,
Dyspareunia,
Swelling, difficulty retracting prepuce.

SIGNS
Patchy or general redness,
Punctate papulovesicles,
Erosions, when severe,
Fissures, cracks, oedema or tightness of prepuce,
Watery, white or purulent subpreputial discharge.

Yeasts, especially *Candida albicans*, are the most common organisms associated with balanitis and the characteristic features include:
redness,
punctate papulovesicles,
white exudate,
oedema,
cracks and fissures of prepuce.

T. vaginalis is a rare cause of balanitis in whites, but is more common in Negroes. The features include:
    redness,
    erosions,
    mucoid or purulent discharge.

Bacterial infection, especially with Vincent's organisms or anaerobes, may produce severe balanitis with:
    marked redness,
    erosions.

Investigations

These, as mentioned in Chapter 3, include:
    smear for Gram stain for leucocytes and yeasts,
    culture for candida species,
    wet film for trichomonads,
    culture for trichomonads,
    swabs for aerobic and anaerobic bacteria,
    where indicated, namely where there are ulcers, culture
      for:
        herpes virus,
        H. ducreyi,
        and dark-ground examinations for *T. pallidum.*

Diagnosis

This rests on the clinical appearance. The cause, if identified, depends on the results of investigations.

Treatment

This includes:
    saline washes,
    nystatin cream for candidal infection,
    metronidazole for trichomonal infection,
    co-trimoxazole,
    dorsal slit,
    circumcision.

Saline washes or bathing favour healing in many cases. If the prepuce retracts, advise thorough cleaning with normal saline, then bathing for 5–10 minutes 2–4 times daily. If the prepuce does not retract, instruct the patient in the technique of irrigating the sub-preputial space with saline using a soft plastic catheter attached to a syringe. Recommend that irrigations are continued until the fluid drains entirely clear, and that the procedure is repeated 2–4 times daily. A heaped teaspoonful of table salt dissolved in a pint of water makes a suitable solution which approximates normal saline.

Nystatin cream. When yeasts are identified, advise a thin smear of nystatin cream after saline bathing.

Metronidazole
> 2 g in a single dose, or
> 400 mg twice a day for 5 days,

is indicated for anyone in whom *T. vaginalis* is identified.

Co-trimoxazole. Give two tablets twice a day for 7 days for the more severe non-candidal, non-trichomonal forms. Avoid antitreponemal antimicrobials.

Dorsal slit may be required for the occasional case with a tight non-retractable prepuce and not responding to the above measures. Circumcision must be performed when all inflammation has resolved.

Circumcision should be considered for anyone with:
> phimosis,
> tight prepuce.

Follow-up

When there are erosions, see monthly for 3 months; at each visit examine, and repeat serological tests (VDRL and TPHA).

When there are no erosions, see 3 months after presentation; examine, and repeat VDRL and TPHA tests.

Complications

These include:
> phimosis,
> paraphimosis,
> phagedena.

Phimosis and paraphimosis may require a dorsal slit and need circumcision. Phagedena demands bacteriological culture, co-trimoxazole and vigorous local saline therapy; later antimicrobial therapy can be adjusted according to the bacteriological findings.

Differential diagnosis

See Table 17.2.

TABLE 17.2   Differential diagnosis of balanitis and balanoposthitis.

Condition	Methods	
Herpes simplex	Appearance	Viral culture (Chapter 14)
Chancroid	History	Bacterial culture (Chapter 16),
Circinate balanitis,	Appearance	Other features of Reiter's disease (Chapter 11),
Balanitis xerotica obliterans,		
Plasma cell balanitis of Zoon,	Appearance	Histology
Pre-malignant conditions,		

Balanitis xerotica obliterans

This is believed to be a genital manifestation of lichen sclerosis et atrophicus. The aetiology is not known. It is commonly first diagnosed in men aged 20–40 years. A similar condition is diagnosed in the vulva and in the female it commonly presents at or after the menopause. It occasionally may be pre-malignant but there is authorative evidence that this is not generally so.

Clinical features

In men this condition affects the:

>   glans, especially around the meatus,
>   prepuce, distally,
>   scrotum, only rarely.

There may be a little irritation. Initially, there is persistent patchy redness sometimes with petechiae and telangiectasia. Later there is atrophy, depigmentation and shrinking with petechiae and telangiectasia sometimes persisting at the margins of the atrophic area. The shrinking can lead to phimosis and meatal stenosis.

In women lichen sclerosis et atrophicus often produces more irritation initially and as well as the vulva, the perineum and anus may be involved. At first, there is redness followed by atrophy, and shrinking can lead to introital stenosis.

Investigations

Biopsy and histology confirm a clinical diagnosis. Usually this is delayed until surgery such as circumcision is indicated.

Diagnosis

This is based on:
> clinical appearance,
> failure of the early balanitis to respond to saline bathing,
> biopsy and histology.

Treatment

This comprises:
> saline bathing,
> topical steroids reduce irritation, but use sparingly or they cause atrophy,
> intra-lesional steroid injections may delay shrinking,
> observation.

Subsequently:
> circumcision for phimosis,
> dilatation for meatal narrowing,
> meatoplasty for persistent severe meatal narrowing.

Prognosis and follow-up

Atrophy and shrinking tend to progress so, as noted above, once the diagnosis is suspected, all cases must be followed by seeing them every 6–12 months.

Complications

As noted above, these include:
> phimosis,
> meatal obstruction.

In addition:
        narrowing may extend up the distal urethra,
        non-gonococcal urethritis may occur.
Note that, provided cases are followed, possible neoplastic change will be detected.

Differential diagnosis

Differentiate from other causes of:
        balanitis,
        phimosis,
        meatal narrowing.

Plasma cell balanitis of Zoon

This is a rare chronic balanitis of unknown origin of middle-aged and elderly men. Moist, shiny, red (usually bright red), patches occur on the glans and under surface of the prepuce. They vary in size and shape with time, and there may be stippling due to haemosiderosis. The diagnosis is made by biopsy and histological examination when marked plasma cell infiltration of the upper cutis is seen. Biopsy should be considered after 3 months in all persisting red lesions of the penis not responding to simple saline bathing. Differentiate from:
        other causes of balanitis,
        pre-malignant conditions, see pages 222 and 224.

Vulvitis

This is usually secondary to vaginitis, especially trichomonal and candidal vaginitis. It may be erythematous or rarely erosive. Always investigate for causes of vaginitis and treat as appropriate. Simple vaginitis usually responds to saline bathing. Differentiate from:
        herpes genitalis,
        acute vulval ulcers of Behçet's syndrome.

Trauma

Trauma may be:
        physical,
        chemical.

Physical trauma

This is rarely diagnosed in STD clinics but trauma commonly occurs during sexual intercourse. Probably many traumatic lesions are invaded by genital micro-organisms and become ulcers. Mentally disturbed patients occasionally inflict physical trauma upon themselves.

Clinical appearances of physical trauma include:
> erythema,
> abrasions,
> cracks,
> fissures,
> lacerations,
> ulcers,
> bruises,
> oedema.

Chemical trauma

This may result from the application of any chemical substance to the genitals. This may be:
> accidental splashing,
> deliberate by a malingerer,
> prophylactic by ill-judged application of strong disinfectants,
> iatrogenic, toxic effects of:
>> podophyllin,
>> trichloracetic acid,
>> cautery.

Clinical appearances are of:
> erythema,
> ulceration.

Investigations

See Table 17.3.

TABLE 17.3   Investigations in cases of suspected genital trauma.

In all cases	Blood for serological tests (VDRL and TPHA).
In appropriate cases	Dark grounds for *T. pallidum*, Culture for herpes simplex virus, Smears and cultures for yeasts, Bacterial culture.

Diagnosis

This rests on:
    clinical appearance,
    exclusions of other conditions by the investigations listed
      above,
A careful history is necessary to identify the occasional patient who deliberately traumatises himself.

Treatment

This comprises:
    saline washes,
    co-trimoxazole when there is marked secondary infection,
    avoid antitreponemal antimicrobials.

Follow-up

Patients should be followed for 3 months. When ulcers or other lesions resembling primary or secondary syphilis are present see monthly for 3 months. In other cases see 3 months after the first attendance.
    At each visit:
      examine,
      take blood for serological tests (VDRL and TPHA).

Complications

    Secondary infection,
    phimosis.

Differential diagnosis

Differentiate from other causes of:
    balanitis,
    ulceration.

Furuncles

Furuncles resulting from pyogenic infection of hair follicles on or near the genitals may present either as typical white papules or may burst leaving a small ulcer. There may be associated inguinal lymph node enlargement.

The diagnosis depends on the clinical appearance and exclusion of other causes of ulceration if present.

Treat with saline bathing and when very infected with co-trimoxazole. Avoid antitreponemal antimicrobials.

Follow-up for 3 months as indicated in the previous section.

Tumours of the genitals

BENIGN TUMOURS

See Table 17.4.

TABLE 17.4   Benign tumours of the genitals.

Tumours appearing anywhere on genitals	Condyloma acuminata, Haemangiomas of all types, Pigmented naevi (moles), Buschke–Lowenstein tumours.
Tumours of penis	Papillae (see p. 237),
Tumours of scrotal wall	Angiokeratoma, Fibroma, Lipoma, Dermoid cysts.
Tumours of vulva	Papillae, Fibroma, Lipoma.

Benign tumours appearing anywhere on the genitals

Condyloma acuminata and *Buschke–Lowenstein tumours* have been considered in Chapter 14.

Haemangiomas of all types may appear anywhere on the external genitalia and may extend into the vagina and rectum. Usually they need no treatment.

Pigmented naevi are common and usually need no treatment. If there is any suggestion of malignant change, refer the patient urgently to a surgeon.

Benign tumours of the scrotal wall

Angiokeratomas are the most common of the haemangiomas so have been listed separately here. They have a warty appearance with telangiectasis. Large ones should be surgically removed.

Fibromas appear as firm painless nodules which may develop peduncles.

Some are neurofibromas, distinguished by their sensitivity to pressure, association with multiple lesions and 'cafe au lait' pigmented patches elsewhere on the skin.

Genital lesions causing symptoms such as pain or inconvenience due to a long peduncle should be surgically removed.

Lipomas are soft, slowly growing, painless lumps only found in the scrotal walls. They may appear fluctuant but have a definite edge. Large tumours need surgical removal.

Dermoid cysts tend to arise under the root of the penis and along the midline. They too should be surgically removed.

Benign vulval tumours

Fibromas and lipomas of the vulva resemble those seen on the scrotal wall. When necessary they should be removed by a gynaecologist.

Pre-malignant conditions

Under this heading are included:
>erythroplasia of Queyrat,
>Bowen's disease,
>Paget's disease
>(For leukoplakia see next sub-section).

All are more commonly diagnosed in men than in women.

The first three are all intraepidermal carcinomas, and can only be differentiated histologically. They present as:

a red patch, which may be:

> raised,
> scaly,
> eczematous,
> moist

ulceration indicates progression to frank carcinoma.

The more common sites for these lesions are shown in Table 17.5.

TABLE 17.5   More common sites of pre-malignant conditions of the genitals.

Condition	Sites
Erythroplasia of Queyrat,	Glans penis Coronal sulcus, Vulva.
Bowen's disease	Penis, Vulva, Perianal region.
Paget's disease	Anywhere on genitals, Very rarely on perineum and perianal region.

Diagnosis depends on:

> clinical appearance,
> persistence of the lesions,
> biopsy and histology.

Treatment is initially saline bathing. Lack of response indicates need for biopsy but it is normal practice to continue saline bathing for about 3 months, if the lesions are static, before biopsy. If the lesions enlarge, biopsy must be done sooner.

Complications. The prime complication is malignant change indicated by:

> rapid enlargement or ulceration,
> urgent biopsy is indicated.

The only other common complication is secondary infection.

Differentiate from chronic balanitis such as:
    plasma cell balanitis of Zoon.

Leukoplakia. This premalignant condition must be considered in the differential diagnosis of any persistent white patches on the genitals. It is found in older patients. Suspect this diagnosis from the appearance and persistence; it is established by biopsy. Treatment is by excision.

Malignant tumours

The common malignant tumours seen in patients attending STD clinics are:
    squamous cell carcinoma,
and less commonly:
    basal cell carcinoma
  Remember:
    connective tissue tumours and secondary deposits also occur.

Clinical features

Carcinomas start as:
    little nodules,
    plaques,
    wart-like lesions.
They usually ulcerate quickly. Occasionally, a squamous cell carcinoma may develop into a fungating lesion.

Diagnosis

This may be suspected from:
        the age of the patient, usually, but not always, older than most
            STD clinic patients,
        the appearance,
        the hardness, compared with that of condyloma acuminata for
            example,
        the persistence.

Investigations

        Exclude STDs rapidly,
        refer to a urologist for biopsy.

Treatment

This is by various combinations of surgery and radiotherapy.

Differential diagnosis

This includes all the causes of genital ulceration already mentioned, but especially:
>   primary syphilis (Chapter 4),
>   herpes simplex (Chapter 14),
>   traumatic ulceration.

Behçet's syndrome

This is a chronic, relapsing disease of unknown aetiology with:
>   oral ulcers,
>   genital ulcers,
>   eye inflammation,
>   lesions in other systems.

It usually starts between the ages of 20 and 30 years and is common in:
>   Middle East,
>   Japan.

Men are affected more than women.

Clinical features

These are listed in Table 17.6.

TABLE 17.6 Clinical features of Behçet's syndrome.

More common features	Less common features
Oral ulcers	Arthritis
Genital ulcers	Venous thrombosis
Eye inflammation:	Epididymitis
Conjunctivitis	Interstitial ulceration
Iritis with hypopyon	Aortic aneurysm
Scleritis	Aortic regurgitation
Keratitis	Cerebral involvement
Retinitis	
Optic neuritis	

Oral ulcers often appear first. They:
    are painful,
    resemble aphthous ulcers,
    may be deep.

Genital ulcers are common on:
    scrotum,
    labia majora.
They may:
    appear anywhere,
    vary from a few mm to 10 mm in diameter,
    tend to be painful,
    heal with atrophic scars, often called 'splash scars' because of
        their appearance.

  In the female, the ulcers have in the past been called 'acute vulval ulcers of Lipschutz'. Ulcers may be restricted to the mouth and genitals for years occurring in bouts, but usually there is gradual worsening. Occasionally, there is improvement in middle age.

Treatment

There is no specific treatment. Apply topical steroids to:
    oral ulcers,
    genital ulcers,
    conjunctivitis.
Refer patients with more severe eye disease to an ophthalmologist, especially if there is a suggestion of impaired vision. An alternative to steroids is immunosuppressive therapy with azothiaprine or chlorambucil either alone or with steroids.

Differential diagnosis

Differentiate from:
    Stevens–Johnson syndrome,
    Reiter's disease (Chapter 11),
    primary and secondary syphilis (Chapter 4),
    hand, foot and mouth disease,
    all the other causes of genital ulcers.

Stevens–Johnson syndrome

This is another disease with oral and genital ulceration. It is probably a variant of erythema multiforme and mainly affects:
   children, and
   young adults.
   Males are affected twice as commonly as females.
   The cause is not known but the disease may develop as a reaction to drugs such as sulphonamides.

Clinical features

The onset is usually acute with fever. Aphthous ulcers occur on the mucosa of the:
   mouth and fauces,
   respiratory tract,
   genital mucosa, including the urethra, producing non-gonococcal urethritis.
   Conjunctivitis, and occasionally, keratitis occur.
   Papular and vesicular skin rashes develop.
   The course is usually 2–3 weeks.

Investigations

Laboratory investigations are usually unhelpful with no specific organisms isolated. The ESR is usually elevated.

Treatment

This is basically rest. Symptomatic measures include:
   steroid eye drops or eye ointment,
   local steroids may also ease the pain or discomfort of other lesions,
   systemic steroids may occasionally be required, usually only for a short course e.g. for severe eye disease.

Differential diagnosis

Differentiate from:
   Behçet's syndrome,
   Reiter's disease (Chapter 11),

primary and secondary syphilis (Chapter 4),
hand, foot and mouth disease,
all the other causes of genital ulcers.

Tuberculosis

Tuberculosis is:
very rare in developed countries,
more common in less developed countries.
After about a week, direct infection may produce a nodule or pustule which soon ulcerates. These appear anywhere on the:
penis,
scrotum,
vulva.
The ulcer:
is tender,
has an irregular undermined edge.
The inguinal lymph nodes are enlarged, may suppurate, and may rarely be the main feature.

Diagnosis

Diagnose by culturing *Mycobacterium tuberculosis*. In the West, biopsy is often done before tuberculosis is suspected.

Treatment

This is by antituberculous chemotherapy supervised by a tuberculosis specialist.

Differential diagnosis

Consider tuberculosis in the differential diagnosis of any genital ulcer:
presenting in a less developed country,
when the patient has recently visited such a country,
when a contact was in a less developed country,
when a contact has visited such a country.
Even rarer forms of genital tuberulosis include:
lesions resembling lupus vulgaris and scrofuloderma,
tuberculous epididymitis,
tuberculous prostatitis.

The last two may occur alone, or associated with tuberculosis elsewhere in the genitourinary tract.

Non-ulcerative conditions

Common skin conditions affecting the genitals

These conditions are not sexually transmitted in the sense that an infective agent such as a micro-organism is acquired and causes disease. The trauma or physical irritation of intercourse may play a part in their aetiology, or chemicals such as those in spermicidal creams may cause irritation.

Seborrhoeic dermatitis

Aetiology

The causes of this condition is undetermined but there are indications that it may be an infective agent.

Features

The skin of the genitalia and perineum of either sex may be affected. Lesions comprise pink scaly patches which may have an indefinite margin. Lesions occur elsewhere on the body either affecting the midline or flexures, including the:

> pre-sternal area,
> interscapular area,
> supra-pubic area,
> natal cleft,
> flexures behind the ears,
> flexures in the groins,
> in addition, dandruff often affects the hair on the head.

Lesions in the midline of the trunk resemble those on the genitalia though some have a brownish colour. Flexural lesions are more linear, lying along the line of the flexure.

Diagnosis

Diagnose from the:

> clinical appearance,
> distribution of lesions.

Treatment

Treat skin lesions with 1 per cent hydrocortisone cream twice daily. Advise regular shampooing for dandruff. A shampoo containing selenium sulphide is usually effective.

Differential diagnosis

Differentiate from the conditions shown in Table 17.7.

TABLE 17.7   Differential diagnosis of common skin conditions affecting genitals, perineum and perianal area.

Tinea,
Candidosis,
Psoriasis,
Seborrhoeic dermatitis,
Flexural dermatitis,
Contact dermatitis,
Secondary syphilis (Chapter 4).
And less commonly:
Pityriasis rosea,
Pityriasis vesicolor.

Tinea cruris

This condition is much more common in men than in women. Patches may affect the skin of the genitals as well as the groins.

Aetiology

Tinea cruris is commonly due to:
epidermophyton floccosum,
trichophyton rubrum.
Poor hygiene and mild trauma may be predisposing factors.

Clinical features

Irritating patches develop in the groins or on the skin of the genitals. They tend to heal centrally and spread peripherally. They are scaly, especially at the periphery where little vesicles or pustules may be present.

Investigations

Skin scrapings. Scrape scales off the lesions on to a slide, mix with dilute (5–10 per cent) potassium hydroxide solution, wait a few minutes and examine under the microscope when the strands of mycelium can be seen.

Diagnosis

Diagnose from the:
    clinical appearance,
    results of skin scrapings.

Treatment

Treat as follows:
    keep the affected area cool and dry,
    apply a fungicide twice daily. These include:
        benzoic acid compound ointment (Whitfield's ointment),
        clotrimazole cream.
It is important to apply the cream or ointment regularly until the lesions entirely disappear and then to continue for at least another 2 weeks.

In severe, resistant, or recurrent cases, consider prescribing griseofulvin 500 mg twice a day by mouth. Give griseofulvin if other structures, such as the nails, are affected. Continue griseofulvin for 6 weeks when only skin is involved, but much longer, up to a year, when the nails are affected. A dermatologist should supervise such cases.

Differential diagnosis

Differentiate from the conditions shown in Table 17.7.

Cutaneous candidosis

Candidosis may affect the skin of the genitals, groins, perineum and perianal region.

Aetiology

Candida albicans and, less commonly, other yeast-like fungi are the predisposing organisms. Poor hygiene and mild trauma may be factors.

Features

Pink, scaly, itchy patches affect the genitals, groins, perineum and perianal regions. Patches are small, diameter about 0·5 cm, initially but coalesce to produce larger lesions; these have a characteristic irregular margin.

Investigations

Scrapings or Gram stain from a swab show characteristic yeast elements which can also be grown on Sabouraud culture medium.

Diagnosis

> Clinical appearance,
> results of scrapings or swab.

Treatment

> Keep the affected area cool and dry. Loose cotton clothing is better than tight garments made of artificial fibres,
> apply nystatin or clotrimazole cream twice daily; choose the latter when there is doubt if the diagnosis is candidosis or tinea,
> continue for at least 2 weeks after all the lesions have disappeared.

Differential diagnosis

Differentiate from the conditions shown in Table 17.7.

Complications

There may also be an element of dermatitis which only resolves if 1 per cent hydrocortisone cream is given as well as the fungicide.

Psoriasis

This is a common skin condition of undetermined aetiology.

Clinical features

Lesions on the genitals may affect the:
    penis,
    scrotum,
    vulva,
and in addition, the:
    pubic area,
    groins,
    perineum.
    Lesions in dry areas of skin consist of flat patches, usually dull red or pink, and scaly. Occasionally, they are smaller and papular. In moist areas, they appear as red shiny patches without scales.
    Skin lesions may also affect the:
        extensor surface of knees and elbows,
        scalp, sometimes only the margin of the hair,
        nails, which show pitting and irregularity.

Diagnosis

Diagnose from the appearance and distribution of the lesions.

Treatment

There is no specific therapy. Treat genital lesions with 1 per cent hydrocortisone cream twice a day. When there are widespread lesions refer the patient to a dermatologist.

Complications

Some cases develop a characteristic polyarthropathy.

Differential diagnosis

Differentiate genital and nearby lesions from the conditions shown in Table 17.7, especially seborrhoeic dermatitis and tinea. When there is arthropathy remember Reiter's disease (Chapter 11) and other causes of polyarthropathy.

Contact dermatitis

Contact dermatitis of the genitals is a relatively rare form of contact dermatitis.

Aetiology

This includes reactions to:
> rubber and chemicals in condoms,
> antiseptics in the bath, soap, sprays and sanitary pads,
> medications used for vaginitis,
> dust penetrating trousers in, for example, carpenters.

Occasionally, allergens may be carried by the hands, including:
> medicaments,
> primula,
> chemicals.

Clinical features

The intensity of the lesions depends on exposure and sensitivity The patient may complain of:
> itch, which may be intense,
> irritation.

Early signs include:
> erythema,
> oedema,
> papules.

Later, there may be:
> dryness,
> scaling,
> thickening.

The erythema varies from mild to intense, the oedema is mild but the papules may become vesicular and burst leaving a weeping surface. The lesions may spread beyond the area of original contact. In the later stages, as well as thickening, there may be lichenification and fissures.

Diagnosis

This depends on attention to the history and the clinical appearance.

Treatment

Treatment is primarily removal of the cause, and explanation to the patient of the cause. A little 1 per cent hydrocortisone cream twice a day may then aid resolution.

Differential diagnosis

Differentiate from the conditions shown in Table 17.7.

Lichen planus

This is a common skin condition of unknown aetiology; it is not infectious but psychological factors may be contributory. Lesions sometimes appear on the genitals in men or the vulva or perianal region in women. On skin they are usually shiny, violet, polygonal flat papules; occasionally they may be annular. On the moist subpreputial area they may be white. Occasionally they itch. Skin lesions also occur on the legs, forearms or wrists and on pigmented skins they may be very dark in colour. A useful clue to the diagnosis is the frequent presence of silvery lesions on the mucous membranes of the mouth.

There is no specific treatment but the disease is self-limiting, lesions disappearing after a few months.

Differential diagnosis

Differentiate from:
    balanitis,
    premalignant conditions,
    secondary syphilis (Chapter 4).

Nodular conditions

Peyronie's disease

This is a rare disease of undetermined cause which develops in middle-aged men. Plaques or nodules of fibrosis arise in the dorsal part of the septum of the penis.

Clinical features

The patient usually presents complaining of:
>   pain in the penis,
>   difficulty with erection and intercourse due to a bend in the erect penis, which may be in any direction.

On examination, a nodule about 0·5 cm in diameter can be felt in the midline of the dorsum of the shaft of the penis. It may be slightly tender in the early stages.

Diagnosis

Diagnose from the:
>   history,
>   palpable nodule.

Treatment

The natural history of Peyronie's disease is for spontaneous improvement to occur, though it takes a long time. This must be remembered in assessing the value of any treatment. Probably, the most important measure is reassurance; if this is accepted, improvement in pain is more likely to follow. Other measures which have been tried include:
>   excision,
>   irradiation,
>   ultrasound,
>   vitamin E by mouth and local corticosteroid injections.

Probably, they have little, if any, effect. Rarely, excision may be indicated in men with persisting marked difficulty with intercourse.

Complications

These include:
>   calcification and ossification of the lesions,
>   Dupuytren's contracture occurs in about 10 per cent of cases.

Differential diagnosis

Differentiate from:
dorsal vein thrombosis,
lymphocoele,
gumma (Chapter 6).

Lymphocoele

This condition is also called sclerosing lymphangitis of the penis. It appears to be due to temporary obstruction of the lymphatics. It may follow prolonged, energetic or frequent intercourse, or it may be associated with another genital lesion, but frequently there is no association except recent but apparently unremarkable intercourse.

The lesion consists of a non-tender cord-like smooth swelling in or near the coronal sulcus parallel to the corona of the glans. This resolves within a few weeks and the only therapy required is reassurance.

Papillae

These are also called pearly penile papules. Histologically, they are keratoangiomas. They tend to develop during the late teens or 20s. They appear as pinhead-sized, pink papules of similar size and shape, arranged in neat rows around the coronal sulcus or corona of the glans. Larger ones develop in the coronal sulcus on either side of the fraenum; apart from these, the size, shape, regularity and arrangement in rows is diagnostic. The only treatment required is reassurance of the occasional adolescent who presents having just noticed them.

Papillae also develop on the inner aspect of the labia minora. They lack the linear arrangement of papillae in the male, but their uniform size and shape is the clue to the diagnosis.

Differential diagnosis

Differentiate from:
warts, which lack the uniformity of size, shape and arrangement (Chapter 14),
sebaceous cysts; clusters of tiny cysts appear on the underside of the prepuce and are rare,

xanthomas; clusters of tiny yellow papules, genital xanthomas
are very rare.

Sebaceous cysts

Sebaceous cysts are common on the genitals, appearing on the:
scrotum,
penile shaft,
underside of the prepuce,
vulva.

Scrotal sebaceous cysts vary in diameter from 2 to nearly 10 mm.
Even larger ones rarely need removal.

Most men have sebaceous cysts on the ventral surface of the
penile shaft. They are only about 2 mm in diameter. An occasional
patient notices them and presents with anxiety; all he needs is
reassurance.

Tiny sebaceous cysts may appear on the under surface of the
prepuce related to ectopic sebaceous glands. No treatment is
needed.

Differential diagnosis

Differentiate from:
warts (Chapter 14),
papillae,
xanthomas.

Dorsal vein thrombosis

Patients occasionally attend with thrombosis of the dorsal vein of
the penis.

Aetiology

This condition may arise following unusually prolonged, energetic
or frequent intercourse, but often appears to follow unremarkable
intercourse. Always consider the possibility of underlying serious
disease such as neoplasia or haematological disorder.

Clinical features

There is cord-like thickening of the proximal part of the dorsal vein of the penis, which may be tender and there may be little oedema of the penis distally.

Treatment

None is required, beyond observation to ensure satisfactory resolution and to exclude serious underlying disease. Advise no intercourse until resolution is complete.

Differential diagnosis

Differentiate from:
    Peyronie's disease,
    gumma.

Some scrotal conditions

The conditions considered here include;
    hydrocoele,
    varicocoele,
    spermatocoele or epididymal cyst,
    haematocoele.

Hydrocoele

Hydrocoele of the tunica vaginalis is associated with:
    gonococcal or non-gonococcal epididymitis,
    tumours or other inflammatory disease of testes or
      epididymes,
    more widespread oedema.

Clinical features

The patient may complain of pain or swelling of scrotum. The condition is almost always unilateral with an obvious swelling and sometimes with redness of the scrotal wall if there is an underlying acute inflammatory lesion. If the swelling is only slight or moderate the scrotal contents may be palpable and any lesion of the contents felt. If the swelling is marked, it may be too tense to allow palpation of the contents. The fact that it is a fluid containing hydrocoele as opposed to other causes of swelling may be shown by transillumination. In addition, it may be distinguished from a hernia by the fact that one can feel the top of the swelling below the external inguinal ring, it can be turned up towards the anterior abdominal wall without pain, there is no cough impulse, and it cannot be reduced like a hernia.

Treatment

Treat any underlying condition, such as epididymitis. In the absence of any such condition, refer to a urologist for aspiration and further assessment.

Differential diagnosis

Differentiate from:
> haematocoele; similar but no transillumination and there may be a history of trauma,
> inguinal hernia; by examination as indicated above,
> solid tumour; by its consistency.

Haematocoele

Blood in the tunica vaginalis is due to trauma or haematological disease. It resembles a hydrocoele as indicated above. Suspected cases should be referred to a urologist for, if neglected, clotting, thickening, fibrosis and even calcification may develop.

Varicocoele

This condition is due to varicocity of the veins in the pampiniform plexus, it is found in young adults, and may be associated with varicose veins in the legs. If it appears in an older patient, it may be related to a tumour obstructing the renal vein.

Clinical features

The condition may be symptomless or there may be dragging pain or discomfort. The condition is nearly always left sided, very occasionally it may be bilateral. On palpation with the patient standing, there is a feeling of a 'bag of worms' in the upper part of the scrotum. When large it may extend down behind the testes. The swelling disappears when the patient lies flat.

Treatment

Often nothing is required.

A suspensory bandage or supporting underpants relieves mild discomfort. Excision is occasionally indicated for marked pain or oligospermia which may lead to subfertility.

Complications

As indicated above, the occasional case is complicated with oligospermia and subfertility. Excision is indicated in these cases.

Spermatocoele

Single or multiple swellings are occasionally found in the upper part of the epididymis. They are due to retention cysts. No treatment is required unless they are large, when aspiration or excision may be indicated.

Oedematous conditions

Genital oedema

Generalised genital oedema may be part of generalised oedema due to:

    cardiac,
    renal,
    nutritional causes,

or may be part of:

    angioneurotic oedema.

Localised genital oedema may be associated with:

    ulcers, or
    dermatitis.

Penile oedema may arise in association with:

    urethral gonorrhoea,

rarely, non-gonococcal urethritis and other intraurethral
conditions,

paraphimosis, and to a lesser extent, phimosis,

dorsal vein thrombosis.

Penile oedema may follow prolonged, frequent or energetic
intercourse and occasionally masturbation. The last relationship
may be the most common, though the relation with masturbation
and intercourse is not clear. Whenever a patient does present with
penile oedema, it is important to consider the other conditions
listed. Whenever there is phimosis with oedema, consider the
possibility of an underlying lesion like primary syphilis or
carcinoma. Dorsal vein thrombosis may occur without oedema.

Treat any underlying cause and recommend supportive
underpants. Follow patients carefully to ensure no underlying
condition is overlooked.

Vulval oedema. Isolated vulval oedema is less marked than penile
oedema. It may be associated with:

candidosis,

bartholinitis (Chapter 8),

trauma due to intercourse,

ulcers, such as primary syphilis (Chapter 4).

Treat any underlying condition, advise saline bathing and follow
carefully.

Lymphoedema

Lymphatic obstruction leading to lymphoedema of the genitals may
be due to:

filariasis,

lymphogranuloma venereum (LGV) (Chapter 16),

granuloma inguinale (Chapter 16),

neoplastic conditions.

Filariasis is the classical cause of marked lymphoedema or
elephantiasis; the lymphoedema of the other conditions is usually
only mild or moderate. Granuloma inguinale rarely causes
lymphoedema, while lymphoedema due to neoplasia varies
according to the neoplastic process.

CHAPTER 18

Non-venereal treponemal conditions

Yaws, endemic syphilis and pinta

These conditions are caused by treponemes morphologically indistinguishable from *T. pallidum* which causes venereal syphilis. The organism which causes yaws is called *Treponema pertenue*. *Treponema pallidum* causes endemic syphilis and *Treponema carateum* causes pinta.

They are all spread by non-sexual contact mainly among children, in primitive communities. They are often called the *endemic treponemal diseases of childhood*. Yaws is the most widespread and probably at one time occurred in many areas in the tropical belt (see map, Fig. 18.1). It was almost eradicated by large WHO campaigns after World War II, but foci have reappeared in primitive communities. Endemic syphilis is found in a few areas north of the tropical belt (map), while pinta is confined to Central America and Northern South America (map).

Yaws

Infection is by direct contact between children during play, often via minor trauma to the legs. The stages are similar to venereal syphilis.

Clinical features

Initial lesion develops at the site of entry, often papillomatous or ulceropapillomatous, and may take weeks or months to heal with scarring.

Early or secondary stage follows. Characteristically, there is a

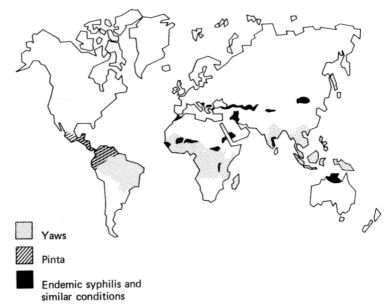

FIG. 18.1 Geographical distribution of non-venereal treponemal diseases.

Yaws

Pinta

Endemic syphilis and similar conditions

rash with papules or papillomas. There is also osteoperiostosis, hydrarthrosis and lymphadenopathy.

Late stage. Gummas develop resembling syphilitic gummas and healing similar scars. Osteoperiostosis, hydrarthosis and bursitis also occur. Destruction of palate, nasal septum and nasal bones producing mutilation called gangosa or rhinopharyngitis mutilans, and hyperkeratosis of soles and palms may all be found.

Latency. As in syphilis, there are long periods of latency.

There is probably no transplacental spread and no CVS or CNS disease.

Diagnosis

This depends on the features listed in Table 18.1.

Treatment

Give a single dose of long-acting benzathine penicillin 2·4–4·8

TABLE 18.1   Diagnosis of yaws.

Country of birth,
Clinical features,
Serological tests:
   Behave as in syphilis,
   VDRL titres remain low.
Normal CSF,
Absence of aortic dilatation or calcification,
Radiographs of bones where indicated.

megaunits i.m. Often, although it is almost certain the patient has yaws, it is wise to treat as for syphilis.

Differential diagnosis

See Table 18.2.

TABLE 18.2   Differential diagnosis of yaws.

Differentiate from:
   Venereal syphilis,
   Endemic syphilis,
   Pinta.

The most important differentiation is from venereal syphilis. Patients who have had yaws:
   may know that they have had yaws (about 50 per cent),
   come from rural communities (about 75 per cent),
   show old periostosis, especially of the tibia (more often in African Negroes than in other groups).

Endemic syphilis

Infection is generally spread from mouth-to-mouth either directly or by sharing eating or drinking utensils in primitive communities. The disease is common in children and among adults in families with infected children.

It was known by different names in different areas, including *bejel* in the upper Euphrates Valley and *firzal* and *loath* elsewhere in the Middle East.

Clinical features

Primary lesions are uncommon and tend to occur around the mouth.

  Secondary stage:
    papular rash, annular and moist papules,
    perianal and genital condylomata lata,
    mucous patches, generalised lymphadenopathy and nocturnal
      bone pains with or without periostosis all occur.
  Late stage:
    there are gummatous lesions of skin, mucosa and bone,
    depigmentation of skin and hyperkeratosis of palms and soles
      may appear,
    long periods of latency also occur,
    there is probably no congenital, CVS or CNS disease.

Diagnosis

Diagnose from features shown in Table 18.3

TABLE 18.3   Diagnosis of endemic syphilis.

Place of birth,
Clinical features,
Serological results,
Normal CSF,
Normal chest radiograph.

Treatment

Benzathine penicillin 2·4 megaunits i.m. If in any doubt, treat as for syphilis.

Differential diagnosis

Differentiate from:
   syphilis,
   yaws,
   pinta.

Pinta

This appears to be the mildest treponemal disease.

Clinical features

Primary lesion or 'pintid' is commonly found on legs, arms or face, starts as a papule but soon spreads to a circular scaly patch; regional lymph nodes are enlarged. The lesions may last for several months.

   Secondary stage. The characteristic feature is a papular rash which may last for several years.

   Late stage:
      lesions on face, hands and feet first,
      hyperpigmentation and then atrophy with hypopigmentation,
      hyperkeratosis of palms and soles occurs,
      bone and aortic lesions are rare; neurological and congenital
         disease probably do not occur; nasopharyngeal ulceration is
         not seen.

Diagnosis and treatment

As outlined for endemic syphilis.

Differential diagnosis

Differentiate from:
      venereal syphilis,
      endemic syphilis,
      yaws.

CHAPTER 19

Diseases found in male homosexuals

Epidemiology

In this chapter the term homosexual is loosely used to cover homosexual and bisexual men. Lesbians rarely present, or are rarely recognised, in STD clinics.

Homosexuals tend to gather in large cities, often in a particular area, such as part of the West End of London. They have their favourite pubs and other meeting places, and in many areas have their own clubs. They often have multiple sexual contacts with little or no knowledge of the identity of their partners. Ignorance of the identity of contacts is often deliberate. Despite the relaxation of laws related to homosexual relations, many sexual encounters remain illegal, even in England. This makes contact tracing difficult and partly explains why there are so many cases of some STDs in this group of men.

Because of the high rates of disease among homosexuals, it is the practice in many clinics to encourage these men to attend regularly every 3–6 months for examination. In addition to clinical examination, the investigations shown in Table 19.1 should be undertaken.

Sites of infection

As shown in Table 19.1, the anorectum and pharynx must be examined and investigated in addition to the urethra in all homosexuals as stated on p. 20. Rectal and pharyngeal infections are often symptom and sign free.

TABLE 19.1   Routine screen for STD in male homosexuals. Repeat every 6 months.

Sample	Investigation
ROUTINE	
Blood	Serum VDRL, TPHA, HBsAg tests,
Rectal secretion	Gram-stain smear for WBC and neisseria-like organisms,
	Culture for *N. gonorrhoeae*,
Throat secretion	Culture for *N. gonorrhoeae*,
Urine	Two-glass test.
WHERE INDICATED BY CLINICAL FEATURES	
Urethral secretion	Gram-stain smear for WBC and neisseria-like organisms,
	Culture for *N. gonorrhoeae*,
Stool	Microscopy for ova and cysts,
	Culture for pathogens.

Infections

Syphilis and gonorrhoea

As stated in Chapter 2, homosexuals have a higher prevalence of primary, secondary and early latent syphilis, and gonorrhoea than heterosexual men. The differences vary but in one survey, syphilis was ten times more prevalent and gonorrhoea three times more prevalent in homosexuals than in heterosexuals.

Methods of diagnosis and treatment of syphilis and gonorrhoea follow the principles already outlined.

Other STDs

In addition to syphilis and gonorrhoea, it is important to consider anorectal, as well as genital sites, for the following condition:

non-specific infection (p. 136),

warts (p. 174),

herpes simplex virus infection (pp. 169 and 170).

Diagnosis and treatment has been described in the relevant chapters.

Inspect the anus in all men for:
    scabies (p. 188),
    pediculosis (p. 191),
    molluscum contagiosum (p. 179),
    and other conditions such as candidosis (p. 165).
Again, diagnosis and treatment follow the principles outlined.
Sometimes, perianal disease in the absence of involvement of other
sites may be the first clue to the sexual orientation of the patient.

Other diseases

As well as the diseases already mentioned, the conditions listed in
Table 19.2 are found in homosexuals. While for the enteric diseases
it is easy to see that oroanal contact readily leads to transfer of

TABLE 19.2   Diseases in male homosexuals
              and bisexuals.

Classic STDs	Syphilis, Gonorrhoea,
Hepatitis B enteric disease	Giardiasis, Amoebiasis, Salmonellosis, Shigellosis, Enterobiasis, Hepatitis A.
Non-A Non-B hepatitis, Anal laceration, Rectal foreign bodies, Anorectal herpes simplex, Anorectal warts.	

organisms, the exact mode of transmission of other conditions is not
understood. The trauma of anorectal intercourse may be an
important factor, for example allowing entry of *T. pallidum* and the
hepatitis B virus. The enteric diseases are more common among
homosexuals in certain major cities in the USA such as New York
and San Francisco than in cities in Britain.

Where these conditions occur in heterosexual men and women,
they are not STDs but spread by the faecal–oral route.

Hepatitis B

The clinical aspects of this disease are covered on p. 181. About 5 per cent of male homosexuals are HBsAg carriers and about 50 per cent have been infected with HBV and have produced antihepatitis B (anti HBs) antibody which is protective. These figures are ten times the value for heterosexual men in Britain.

Both surface antigen (HBsAg) and e antigen (HBeAg—a marker of infectivity) are found in most body fluids including blood, semen and saliva, hence the suggestion that sexual transmission may be related to the anorectal trauma occurring during intercourse.

As indicated on p. 181, the patients have mild or no symptoms, they are rarely jaundiced, serum liver function tests are only slightly abnormal. In contrast, of those who have had liver biopsies, 50 per cent have shown chronic active hepatitis or active cirrhosis.

At present there is no effective treatment. A vaccine is currently under trial and preliminary results are encouraging. In the meantime, warn all HBsAg carriers of their potential infectivity, advise minimal partner change, examine all possible contacts and check all homosexuals every 6–12 months for HBsAg carriage.

Hepatitis A

This appears to be sexually transmitted among male homosexuals. It is described on p. 182.

Enteric disease

Like hepatitis A and B, the enteric diseases listed in Table 19.2 rarely produce clinical disease among homosexuals. They are only detected by examination of the stools. Routine examination of stools has produced very much lower yields in Britain than in cities like New York and San Francisco. Stool examination among homosexuals in Britain is probably only indicated in patients returning from cities like New York or in patients with bowel symptoms, especially if they have visited parts of the world like the Far East where enteric disease is common in all people. Examination of a single stool only detects about 80 per cent of cases; in suspicious cases with negative results to the first stool, repeat the examination. Treatment of enteric diseases is summarised in Table 19.3. Obtain three negative stools after therapy to ensure cure.

TABLE 19.3 Treatment of enteric diseases seen in homosexuals.

Condition	Therapy
Giardiasis	Metronidazole, 800 mg three times a day for 5 days,
Amoebiasis	Metronidazole, 800 mg three times a day for 5 days,
Salmonellosis	Antimicrobial therapy not usually indicated,
Shigellosis	
Enterobiasis	Piperazine, four 500 mg tablets daily for 7 days.

Anal lacerations

Penoanal intercourse readily causes minor and occasionally major anal trauma especially fissure *in-ano* and other lacerations. These traumatic lesions may allow entry of hepatitis B virus and perhaps other pathogens such as *T. pallidum.*

It is important to recognise the origin of anal trauma and screen patients for other STDs.

Rectal foreign bodies

A wide variety of foreign bodies have been extracted from the rectum having been used for sexual gratification. Refer such patients to a proctologist or surgeon for removal of the foreign body, and screen all such patients for STDs.

Anorectal herpes simplex and warts

Anal herpes simplex and warts will be noted during routine clinical examination. Whenever they are seen, proctoscopy should be performed to see if there is rectal involvement. These conditions may be the first indication of homosexuality, and they are described in Chapter 14.

Index